COPING WITH OBSESSIVE-
COMPULSIVE DISORDER

ALSO AVAILABLE IN THE *COPING WITH* SERIES
Series Editor: Steven Jones, University of Lancaster

Coping with Bipolar Disorder:
A CBT-Informed Guide to Living with Manic Depression
Steven Jones, Peter Hayward and Dominic Lam
ISBN 978–1–85168–699–5

Coping with Schizophrenia:
A Guide for Patients, Families and Caregivers
Steven Jones and Peter Hayward
ISBN 978–1–85168–344–4

Coping with an Anxious or Depressed Child:
A Guide for Parents
Sam Cartwright-Hatton
ISBN 978–1–85168–482–3

Coping with Fears and Phobias: A Step-by-Step
Guide to Understanding and Facing your Anxieties
Warren Mansell
ISBN 978–1–85168–514–1

Coping with Shyness and Social Phobia:
A Guide to Understanding and Overcoming Social Anxiety
W. Ray Crozier and Lynn E. Alden
ISBN 978–1–85168–516–5

TO ORDER TITLES
All the titles in this series are available direct from the publisher.
Please visit www.oneworld-publications.com to order books online.

Coping with
Obsessive-Compulsive Disorder
A Step-by-Step Guide Using the Latest CBT Techniques

Jan van Niekerk

ONEWORLD
OXFORD

A Oneworld Paperback Original

Published by Oneworld Publications 2009

ISBN 978–1–85168–515–8

Typeset by Jayvee, Trivandrum, India
Cover design by Mungo Designs
Printed and bound in Great Britain by
Bell & Bain, Glasgow

Oneworld Publications
185 Banbury Road
Oxford OX2 7AR
England
www.oneworld-publications.com

Contents

B. BEHAVIOURAL TRACK

8 Exposure and response prevention therapy   163

PART THREE: STAYING WELL

9 Using a holistic approach   205

10 Taking stock and staying well   218

Appendices

Series Foreword

This series is intended to provide clear, accessible, and practical information to individuals with a wide range of psychological disorders, as well as to their friends, relatives, and interested professionals. As the causes of emotional distress can be complex, books in this series are not designed purely to detail self-treatment information. Instead, each volume sets out to offer guidance on the relevant, evidence-based psychological approaches that are available for the particular condition under discussion. Where appropriate, suggestions are also given on how to apply particular aspects of those techniques that can be incorporated into self-help approaches. Equally important, readers are offered information on which forms of therapy are likely to be beneficial, enabling sufferers to make informed decisions about treatment options with their referring clinician.

Each book also considers aspects of the disorder that are likely to be relevant to each individual's experience of receiving treatment, including the therapeutic approaches of medical professionals, the nature of diagnosis, and the myths that might surround a particular disorder. General issues that can also affect a sufferer's quality of life, such as stigma, isolation, self-care and relationships are also covered in many of the volumes.

The books in this series are not intended to replace therapists, since many individuals will need a personal treatment programme from a qualified clinician. However, each title offers individually tailored strategies, devised by highly experienced practising clinicians, predominantly based on the latest techniques of cognitive-behavioural therapy, which have been shown to be extremely effective in changing the way sufferers think about themselves and their problems. In addition, titles also include a variety of practical features such as rating scales and diary sheets, helpful case studies drawn from real life, and a wide range of up-to-date resources including self-help groups, recommended reading, and useful websites. Consequently, each book provides the necessary materials for sufferers to become active participants in their own care, enabling constructive engagement with clinical professionals when needed and, when appropriate, to take independent action.

Dr Steven Jones
Series Editor

Foreword

A successful self-help book needs to resemble good therapy – identifying the personal nature of the problem, addressing specific and non-specific factors alike, and interacting with the person at their own pace – to provide a learning experience that installs autonomous skills.

Jan van Niekerk's self-help guide for people with obsessive-compulsive disorder (OCD) not only accomplishes all this but contains numerous novel features. The guide begins with a very readable and comprehensive description of OCD to enable readers to recognize themselves and move on to managing the disorder. The author then presents the major current cognitive-behavioural therapy (CBT) models and renders theoretically distinct approaches clinically accessible and blendable through down-to-earth explanations and practical engaging exercises.

The book moves seamlessly through different stages of the therapeutic process covering both the attention to detail necessary for successful application of techniques through to the more holistic level of lifestyle choice and improved overall functioning required to sustain long-term change. Throughout the text the reader is conscious of the presence of the author through personalized advice and comments guiding us over the gradients and troughs of self-control. The reader is never alone, and the presence of the case examples illustrates well the experience of the therapy across different manifestions of OCD and adds to the good company.

I had the pleasure of meeting Jan van Niekerk when he spent a short time with our team in Montreal in the summer of 2006. He had contacted us on his own initiative to follow up on articles he had read on our inference-based approach (IBA) (see O'Connor et al., 2005). This approach developed from our clinical observations that most OCD did not seem to fit a phobic model and the fear was more about what the person inferred might be there than what was there in reality. In OCD, the person concludes that, for example, a hand was dirty or a door not locked or an object was badly placed, on the basis of a subjective story remote from the here-and-now which bypassed the usual information-gathering, a process we term 'inferential confusion'. A more fundamental self-doubt such as 'I could be someone who makes mistakes, does harm, is negligent', may lie behind the specific obsessional doubt; a self-inference also remote from the real self (Aardema and O'Connor, 2007).

Jan van Niekerk describes the IBA procedures (Chapter 5) to identify obsessional doubt and reasoning errors which lead to confusing inferences. But he also integrates IBA along with existing work on inflated responsibility, what the obsessional fears mean about the person, thought–action fusion, the effects of metacognitive control strategies, metacognitive appraisal, the effects of compulsive checking on memory confidence, and response prevention strategies (all in Chapters 5–7). Chapter 8 describes the methods of exposure and response prevention therapy as a stand-alone treatment option, offering the reader a choice between CBT and this older, but powerful treatment approach. In fact, all the therapy techniques sit well together and make this guide a unique up-to-date comprehensive text nicely blending old and new. However, the textbook principles are brought alive by his practical tips, informal asides and pick-me-up helplines, which seem to catch the reader and pull us up just at the right moment to keep motivation and mood high and progress steady.

Overcoming OCD involves not only removing symptoms, but improving life functioning and quality of life. So Jan van Niekerk thoughtfully adds a final section addressing well-being and positive emotions. Jan van Niekerk brings all these diverse CBT approaches sensibly and sensitively together, which makes this book captivating reading for client and professional alike.

Kieron O'Connor, Ph.D., C. Psychol., AFBPsS.
Montreal

Acknowledgements

I would like to thank the following people for discussions that informed the perspectives outlined in this book: my colleagues and trainees in Cambridge, but particularly Kieron O'Connor, Fred Aardema and Marie-Claude Pélissier in Montreal.

I am indebted to Cory Newman and Christine Padesky for past insights gained during the course of outstanding cognitive therapy supervision.

I would like to thank Isobel Dixon for her invaluable editorial assistance and Geraldine Owen for professional support.

Finally, I would like to thank my clients with obsessive-compulsive disorder (OCD), past and present, for allowing me to learn from their experience.

Introduction

Is this book for me?

Consider the following:

- Do you spend more time than most people washing or cleaning, and worry about what might happen if you didn't?
- Do you find yourself being fearful if you haven't checked things a lot?
- Do you have thoughts that pester you, thoughts that you just can't get rid of, no matter how hard you try?
- Do you worry that you might do something impulsively, out of character and against your intention?
- Do you take a very long time to finish tasks and activities, and find it very difficult to speed up?
- Do you feel uneasy or nervous if you didn't arrange items in a specific order or pattern or perform an action in a specific sequence?
- Are any of the above causing problems in your life?

If your answer to any of these questions is 'yes', there is a possibility that you may have a condition called 'obsessive-compulsive disorder', or OCD in short. Your problems may well have left you feeling frustrated, and you may be disheartened about trying to be rid of them. However, the good news is that psychological and medical research over the past decades has made major progress in helping us to understand OCD better, and in developing effective treatments.

In this book I will explain to you what is currently known about OCD and then take you through some self-help strategies step by step. These are ways to overcome this condition or manage it in a way that interferes minimally with your life. You will be introduced to a number of people with OCD and we will follow their progress as they apply these strategies. The views expressed in this book are based on the latest research evidence and also on my clinical experience in working with people with OCD.

PART ONE
BACKGROUND

1

Do I suffer from OCD?

Types of obsessions and compulsions

The definitive symptoms of obsessive-compulsive disorder (OCD) are *obsessions* and *compulsions*, but what do these words mean? Let's first consider what is meant by 'obsession'.

The question is complicated by the ordinary use of the word; for example, if someone spends a lot of time gardening, or watching football, their friends may say that they are *obsessed* with gardening or football. However, mental health professionals use the term differently. Psychologists define obsessions as *repetitive thoughts, images, or impulses* that pester you and that you try to ignore or suppress or try to get rid of in some other way.

Usually people with OCD consider their obsessions to be irrational, and they may feel embarrassed or ashamed about having them but find it exceedingly difficult to ignore them because of the anxiety or other negative feelings they may cause. *Obsessions* can have many different themes, and the following will give you some idea of the range of obsessions experienced in OCD (this list is not exhaustive). Ask yourself which of these may apply to you and bear in mind that the experience of a number of different obsessions is common:

- Fears that you have been contaminated with dirt, germs, bodily secretions, chemicals, or other dangerous materials.
- Fears that you have not locked, closed or turned off something properly (such as your front door or the taps), or that you have left an electrical appliance switched on (e.g. the oven).
- Being very concerned about things being in order or symmetrical or 'just right' (such as that the rug should lie perfectly symmetrically, or an activity should be done exactly according to a set routine).
- Having unwanted thoughts about sexual activity, for example, being a paedophile, or having intercourse with a relative or a religious figure.
- Having thoughts which make it difficult to throw away useless or worn-out items and having strong urges to collect unnecessary or trivial items.
- Having unwanted violent or aggressive thoughts, such as stabbing a vulnerable person.

On the other hand, *compulsions* are *repetitive acts* that you feel compelled to perform. They are aimed at making the situation safe or setting things right and occur in response to obsessions. A compulsion may be behavioural (another person can see you doing it) or mental (you do it in your mind). The urge to perform a compulsion is usually overbearingly strong, and very difficult to resist. The term 'ritual' is sometimes used as a synonym for 'compulsion' and will be used from this point onwards. The following are examples of common compulsions or rituals – think of which of these may apply to you:

- Checking, for example, whether the door is locked or the gas heating turned off.
- Washing and cleaning, for example, scrubbing your hands or cleaning the house.
- Repeating your actions, for example, walking through a doorway twice.
- Quietly saying a prayer or thinking a special word (an example of a mental ritual).
- Carefully thinking thoughts that 'undo' bad or wrong thoughts (a mental ritual).
- Arranging items symmetrically or in an exact order.
- Buying or failing to throw away unnecessary or useless items.
- Counting objects or steps in an activity, sometimes to avoid unlucky numbers.

Who gets obsessions and compulsions?

The answer to this question must seem obvious – people with OCD! But, hang on, it's not that simple. For many years it was thought that the experience of obsessions and rituals was limited to people suffering from OCD. However, we now know that this is not the case. In fact, recent studies have shown that experiences similar to the obsessions and rituals in OCD, but less intense and disruptive, may be relatively commonplace. For example, one study (Rachman and De Silva, 1978) found in a group of 124 students and health professionals, that 99 reported that they had experienced intrusive, unacceptable thoughts and impulses – this translates into almost 80% of the group! A group of 40 was questioned closely about the nature of the intrusive thoughts they experienced, of which some examples are provided in table 1 below. Consider which of these you may have experienced.

Similarly, in a group of 150 university students and employees, 82 (55%) reported that they performed ritualistic actions.

Table 1 Examples of intrusive thoughts experienced by people without OCD

Jumping onto the rails when the tube train is approaching

Saying something nasty and damning to someone

Acts of violence in sex

Something being wrong with her health

Doing something, e.g. shouting or throwing things, to disrupt the peace in a gathering

Harm befalling her children, especially accidents

That the probability of an air-accident to herself would be minimized if a relative had such an accident

An accident, especially a car accident, happening to a loved one

Buying unwanted things

That she, her husband and baby (due) would be greatly harmed because of exposure to asbestos, with conviction that there are tiny asbestos dust particles in the house

Harming, or being violent towards, children – especially smaller ones

Crashing a car when driving

Walking along a crowded passage and suddenly discovering that he is naked

Pushing people away when in a queue

'Unnatural' sexual acts

Wishing that someone close to her was hurt or harmed

Doing something dramatic like trying to rob a bank

In the group of 82, 27% reported checking, 16% reported washing, cleaning and ordering, 6% reported avoiding particular objects, and 51% reported performing 'magical' protective acts (Muris et al., 1997).

Diagnosis of OCD

How do mental health professionals decide whether you have OCD? This is no straightforward matter. As we have seen most people will intermittently have odd, disturbing or unusual thoughts or act in an eccentric or ritualized way. So, when considering the obsessions and rituals you describe to them, professionals face the difficult task of deciding when the problem warrants diagnosis and treatment.

Their way of solving this dilemma is to consider the *extent* of your obsessions and rituals, how much they *interfere* with your life, and how *upsetting* they are to you. In the study described above (Muris et al., 1997), people with OCD found that their obsessions lasted longer than normal intrusive thoughts, and were more discomfiting, intense and frequent. Similarly, OCD rituals were more frequent and intense, were met by more resistance and discomfort, and were more often carried out in response to being upset, than normal rituals. Therefore you are likely to have OCD if these problems leave you feeling helpless and upset, and present an obstacle to getting on with doing the things you want to do. OCD sufferers find that the condition gains a foothold in their lives and increasingly demands more time and effort. You may sense that the OCD is slowly wresting control away from you.

Distinguishing OCD from related conditions

As we have seen, the diagnosis of OCD is not always straightforward. To clarify this further, I will next consider a few conditions that share features with OCD. Before starting treatment it is important to establish which diagnosis best explains your current difficulties. Sometimes a single diagnosis may be sufficient, but it is also possible that certain conditions co-exist. For instance, OCD and depression frequently go hand in hand.

Generalized anxiety disorder and depression

People afflicted with generalized anxiety disorder (GAD) worry disproportionately and anxiously about a wide range of issues for at least six months. On the other hand, the hallmark of a clinical depressive episode (Churchill's 'black dog'), is persistently feeling low and losing interest or not enjoying your usual activities. Typically, any number of the following symptoms add insult to injury in depression: reduced or increased appetite, weight loss or weight gain, difficulty sleeping or wanting to sleep all the time (insomnia or hypersomnia), restlessness or feeling slowed down, tiredness, feeling worthless or guilty, difficulty concentrating or indecisiveness and having frequent thoughts about death or even suicide. Sometimes depression may make it more likely that your OCD symptoms will flare up, and sometimes you may start feeling depressed when you notice how much the OCD has encroached on your life.

Persistent and sometimes intrusive worry thoughts can occur both in depression and GAD. However, the worrying thoughts tend to concern real-life problems, usually with the aim of trying to find a solution or helping to prepare for what can go wrong, or they may simply involve ruminating at length about what is already wrong. In OCD, the person tends to experience obsessions as intrusive and inappropriate. They usually try to resist the thoughts in some way, such as to ignore or suppress them. Or they cope with them in some other way such as by neutralizing them or performing rituals to reassure themselves. However, contrary to GAD or depression, these rituals or neutralizing acts are clearly excessive or extreme and need to be performed in a repetitive way and are not realistically connected with what they aim to prevent.

Health anxiety

People with health anxiety experience repetitive thoughts about having a physical disease based on the misinterpretation of sensations or perceived changes in their body as being evidence of a serious but yet unidentified medical problem. They frequently try to reassure themselves by checking their bodies or asking others, including their GP, for reassurance. However, usually their fears persist despite reassurance that nothing is wrong, or any benefit from reassurance is short-lived until their fears are triggered again. Health anxiety shares a number of features with OCD; for example, frequently there is 'obsessive rumination' about illness and repetitive behaviours (e.g. checking one's body) as an attempt to reduce anxiety. Also, people tend not to be convinced by reassurance. However, the scope of obsessions in OCD tends to be much broader than just concerns about physical illness, and in OCD with germ contamination fears, the concern is about *getting* an illness, while in health anxiety the concern tends to be about *having* an illness.

Obsessive-compulsive personality disorder (OCPD)

The word 'personality' refers to enduring tendencies (or traits) in how a person responds in a variety of situations and in their style of relating to other people, and it tends to remain relatively stable from their mid-20s onwards. For example, some people may tend to be extroverted (vivacious and socially outgoing) and others may tend to be introverted (more quiet and don't socialize as easily). In the case of personality *disorders*, a set of personality characteristics cause an excess of stress or disruption in a person's life, and their ability to relate to others may frequently be compromised.

According to a widely used diagnostic system, people with obsessive-compulsive personality disorder (OCPD) are characterized by a preoccupation with orderliness, perfectionism and attempts at controlling their environment, as part of a pattern that starts in early adulthood. They think rigidly in black and white terms, and expect others to do things according to their rules. They may frequently be overconscientious and live their lives in a highly organized way to the point of 'not seeing the wood for the trees' and, rather than being a means to an end, sticking to the rules and being organized become an end in itself. They tend to control their emotions and behaviour, and others often experience them as somewhat cold and aloof. They prefer routine and predictability, and spurn spontaneity and acting on a whim. Of course, you may notice that many healthy and well-functioning people have some of the characteristics described above; however, in the case of OCPD a defining characteristic is that these features are extreme to the point of causing recurrent problems for themselves or in their dealings with others.

People with OCD may sometimes have features of OCPD, although only a small percentage will have both conditions (about one in five, or fewer; Wu et al., 2006). One major difference is in the degree of life impairment and whether people perceive themselves as needing treatment. People with OCD tend to experience major disruption in their lives (of course, varying according to the level of severity of their OCD). In contrast, people with OCPD will tend not to see a problem with their own behaviour and will rarely feel that they need help – usually the problem is brought to their awareness by the protestations of other people, such as relatives or colleagues, who have been negatively affected by their behaviour.

Tic disorder and Tourette's disorder

People with tic disorder experience uncontrollable repetitive movements (motor tics) or production of sounds (vocal tics). Examples are blinking, lip smacking, facial twitching, shoulder twitches or coughing, grunting or clearing the throat. These can sometimes be difficult to distinguish from OCD rituals; however, in the case of OCD, rituals are usually voluntarily initiated to deal with the psychological discomfort – usually anxiety – caused by obsessions.

Some people may experience repetitive thoughts, in the absence of anxiety or discomfort, such as a song or tune that keeps on playing in their mind, that may best be considered to be a form of mental tic. This is a common experience and not an indication of a disorder as long as there is no serious disruption to the person's life.

Tourette's is a neuropsychiatric disorder that usually starts in early childhood and causes various motor and vocal tics. The person may repeat phrases that he or she hears other people say (echolalia) or have an uncontrollable urge to say obscene things (coprolalia). As we can imagine, this can cause a lot of embarrassment to the sufferer and their loved ones, and also disrupts their lives. Tourette's disorder sometimes co-occurs with OCD.

How common is OCD and what is its course and impact?

Now that we have established how OCD is diagnosed, we can consider what research studies can tell us about the people who suffer from this condition.

We now know that OCD is the fourth most common mental disorder after depression, alcohol and drug abuse, and social phobia (intense anxiety in social situations). About 2–3% of people will suffer from OCD at some point in their lives – this translates to about one in every 50 people.

OCD may start at any age from early childhood to old age, but would typically have its onset in men in the late teenage years and in women in the early 20s. It sometimes, but not always, starts after a stressful event or during stressful circumstances. This does not mean that stress necessarily causes OCD in itself, but more likely means that in people who have a biological and psychological vulnerability to the condition (which we will discuss in more detail later on), certain sources of stress may act as a trigger. Although OCD symptoms can be chronic, they typically wax and wane, and it is a frequent experience that stress, such as work or relationship problems, makes symptoms worse.

No person with OCD has exactly the same symptoms, and the severity of symptoms frequently changes over time as periods of relative calm may be followed by symptoms getting worse again. ('Relapse' is a word that mental health professionals use to describe a re-emergence of symptoms after a period relatively free of symptoms.) The severity of symptoms also differs between people. Therefore the disruption caused by symptoms may range from being an occasional nuisance to causing grave difficulty in the ability to function at work or at home, leading to a major handicap and dependence on support by family or others. It is unfortunate that, despite the availability of effective treatments, many people wait years before seeking help.

OCD and the family

As we have seen, rituals are acts which the person feels a very strong urge to perform. At some point family members may start taking notice of ritualizing despite the person's best attempts at concealment. Some rituals are easier to conceal than others. For example, when you have to triple-check all the electrical appliances in the house, and the door, and the taps before you leave in the morning, this may be pretty obvious to your husband waiting in the car. However, when you carry out a mental ritual like saying a short prayer in response to having a 'bad thought', you may simply seem a bit preoccupied with your thoughts.

Family members may respond to ritualizing in many different ways. They may well take a humorous perspective if the ritualizing is not disruptive and consider this to be harmless and a bit eccentric. Alternatively, they may be concerned about seeing a loved one behaving in such seemingly inexplicable ways. They may be very concerned when they start noticing that a person is distressed at having to do the rituals and having difficulty in getting on at home and at work.

Another worrying situation is where, because of the person's obvious difficulty in resisting the rituals and their insistence on performing them, family members respond by helping their loved one with her rituals or stepping in when the person can't perform certain activities because of their rituals. In this way, the household situation increasingly adjusts itself to accommodate the OCD. As we will see later, while the desire to come to a loved one's assistance in this situation is understandable, it may not be helpful in the long term.

OCD in the media

Frequently the portrayal of OCD in the media can be quite misleading and encourage public misconceptions. People with OCD may be forgiven for being annoyed when ritualizing is portrayed for comic relief, diminishing the distress and disruption that sufferers frequently experience. Ritualizing is sometimes depicted as a very public activity, whereas sufferers commonly go to great lengths to keep ritualizing hidden from scrutiny. This emphasizes the need for public education about OCD. Fortunately, much progress has been made in this respect over the last few decades.

Here are some examples of characters in films and on television apparently suffering from OCD:

- Jack Nicholson's uncouth character Melvin Udall in *As Good As It Gets* (1997) performs ordering and washing rituals. The film has been criticized for portraying OCD in an exaggerated way for getting laughs.
- In the film *The Aviator* (2004) Leonardo di Caprio plays the reclusive genius, Howard Hughes, who had obsessive fears of contamination by germs.
- In Shakespeare's play *Macbeth*, a doctor is called to observe Lady Macbeth because of her repeated handwashing after

because of her guilt at the murder of the king. She famously mutters to herself 'Here's the smell of the blood still … all the perfumes of Arabia will not sweeten this little hand.'

- In the episode *Sense and Senility* of the comedy series *Blackadder*, the two actors who visit the prince have to perform a ritual whenever the real name of 'the Scottish play' (*Macbeth*) is mentioned (perhaps this is an exaggerated manifestation as OCD of the common superstition in the theatre world).

Famous people with OCD

The following famous people or celebrities may suffer or have suffered from OCD:

- Footballer, David Beckham, described having 'this disorder where I have to have everything in a straight line or everything has to be in pairs'. According to his wife, Victoria, 'Everything has to match in the house. If there are three cans of Diet Pepsi, he'd throw one away because it's uneven.'
- Dr Samuel Johnson, eighteenth-century compiler of the first dictionary of the English language, would perform ritualized movements when crossing the threshold of a door. Just before crossing, he would whirl, twist, make a series of hand motions and then leap over the threshold. He would never step on cracks between paving stones and would touch every post he passed. If he missed one he had to go back and touch it.

When to get professional help

So, now you may have established that you suffer from OCD. What next? This book will offer you guidance on the strategies – both psychological and medical – that you can use to overcome this condition. But, there are times when it may be advisable also to consult a mental health professional, either a clinical psychologist or psychotherapist who practises cognitive-behavioural psychotherapy (CBT), and/or a general practitioner or psychiatrist for advice on medication. How do you decide whom to consult and when? The following is a list of questions that may help you decide:

- Has your OCD been associated with feeling consistently low and depressed over recent weeks, to such an extent that you have taken time off work or others have expressed concern about you?
- Has your OCD led you seriously to consider suicide as a way of escaping from your problems, or led you to neglect taking care of yourself to such an extent that people have expressed concern about you?
- Have you regularly taken time off work for OCD-related reasons?
- Has your OCD caused major stress or a breakdown in any of your relationships?

If you answered 'yes' to any one of the above questions, then it would be advisable to seek the help of a mental health professional specialized in the treatment of OCD. You may consider psychological therapy, medication or a combination of the two (the relative merits of CBT versus medication are discussed at the end of Chapter 2).

Psychological treatment

If you have to be referred to a suitable service, perhaps via your GP, it is best to express your preferences about types of treatment at an early stage. An option for identifying a suitably qualified person is to contact national professional associations, which should be able to offer a list of therapists in your area. I would strongly recommend seeing someone with expertise in cognitive-behavioural therapy (CBT) and experience in treating OCD. These may include registered clinical psychologists or cognitive-behavioural psychotherapists. Evidence of expertise in CBT may include a qualification in CBT, such as a diploma or certificate, or specialized training from a reputable institution, or significant experience working in a mental health service specializing in CBT. The therapist should preferably have treated at least five or more people with OCD. If you are unsure about their knowledge or experience, make an appointment to see them and discuss what they can offer you. If you continue to have doubts after such a meeting, better find another therapist.

Medication

Medication has to be prescribed by a medical practitioner, such as your GP. However, particularly if your condition is chronic and severe, it is preferable to be assessed by a psychiatrist with expertise in the treatment of OCD. Your GP will be able to advise you on options for specialized services.

A list of general resources for further support and information is provided in Appendix 1.

Key points

- An obsession is a repetitive thought, image or impulse that you may try to resist.
- Having an obsession results in anxiety or other negative feelings.
- A compulsion or ritual is a repetitive act that you feel compelled to perform to reduce the anxiety caused by an obsession.
- Many people have experiences similar to the obsessions and rituals in OCD, but less intense and disruptive.
- Professionals diagnose OCD when the obsessions and rituals interfere significantly in your life.

- About one in 50 people will suffer from OCD at some point in their lives.
- OCD symptoms tend to fluctuate, and there is a chance of relapse.
- Cognitive-behavioural therapy (CBT) or medication can be effective for the treatment of OCD.

2

What causes OCD and maintains it?

It is impossible to get out of a problem by using the same kind of thinking that it took to get into it.

Albert Einstein

In this chapter I will introduce you to the cognitive-behavioural model, and what this can tell us about OCD. Next will follow an overview of biological theories and treatments of OCD, and I will compare and discuss the pros and cons of medication and psychological therapy. Finally, I will give an outline of how the rest of the book fits together to help you with your OCD.

Cognitive-behavioural therapy (CBT)

People are disturbed not by things, but by the view which they take of them.

Epictetus, Greek philosopher

This ancient quote reflects the main idea behind cognitive-behavioural therapy (CBT). Often, different people will have different thoughts about the same event or experience. The classic example is that of a glass of water filled halfway – one person sees it as half-empty and the other sees it as half-full.

But why does this matter? During or after a situation or event we have automatic thoughts (automatic, because they just pop into your head) about the event. These represent the meaning or interpretation we attach to the event. How we feel (our emotions) and how we choose to respond (behaviour or coping) depend on this meaning. In turn, our emotional response may affect our bodily sensations, for example, when feeling anxious your heart may be thumping and your hands may be clammy and shaky.

Automatic thoughts don't arise in a vacuum. They stem from our *underlying beliefs* about ourselves, other people, the future, the past, and so on, or the *assumptions* we make, or the *rules* we hold ourselves or others to. In turn, our underlying beliefs are influenced by our previous life experiences. This relationship is illustrated in figure 1.

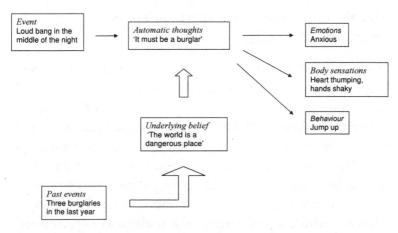

Figure 1 *Situation*: Person lies asleep in bedroom

A few points to clarify

It is important to distinguish thoughts and feelings, as the English language can sometimes confusingly introduce a thought with 'I *feel* that ...' A simple distinction is that to express a thought usually requires a phrase or sentence, and an emotion or feeling usually requires a single word (e.g. happy, sad, frustrated, cheerful, relaxed, angry, bewildered, guilty, ashamed, anxious, upset, depressed, low, and so on).

After thinking about the cognitive-behavioural model, you may retort that emotions sometimes precede thinking, such as when feeling low may cause negative thinking rather than the other way around. This is a valid point, and we have to acknowledge that the relationship between mood and thinking can be complex, and that the one may influence the other. This may result in a *vicious cycle* where negative thoughts cause low mood, and low mood in turn invites further negative thinking, and so on. However, for the purposes of CBT, the important point is that thoughts can influence emotion, mood and behaviour. Next we will consider, more specifically, how the CBT model makes sense of emotional difficulties, and then OCD.

How the CBT model can help us understand emotional difficulties

We have established that the *meanings* we attach to events have consequences for how we feel and how we respond. Sometimes these thoughts may leave us feeling disturbed or distressed, as illustrated in figure 1. Cognitive-behavioural therapists believe that people do not have to continue to interpret events in the same way for the rest of their lives. They can learn to think differently about events and therefore be less upset by them.

Most often we have realistic grounds or good *evidence* for what we believe about others or ourselves. However, sometimes our beliefs may rely on a *biased* or one-sided view of reality, which is a bit like holding a prejudice. A depressed person may remember the person who ignored him but not the ones who chatted to him and conclude, 'Nobody likes me.' In CBT these tendencies are referred to as *thought distortions*, and the problem with this skewed thinking is that by its nature it gives a false view of the world. Here is a list of thought distortions that are common villains leading to prolonged and excessive levels of upset.

Thought distortions

All-or-nothing thinking: the tendency to evaluate your own or other people's performance or personal qualities as black/white. Also called the *fallacy of bifurcation*: presenting only two alternatives where others exist (Pirie, 2006), e.g.

- 'I didn't get the promotion: that means I'm a nobody.'
- 'People are either your friends or your enemies.'
- 'You're either normal or mad.'

The world is *complex*: people or events are usually not just one way or the other. 'Shades of grey' are not acknowledged.

Magnification: a tendency to reach blanket negative conclusions about yourself or other people on the basis of flimsy evidence, e.g.

- After making a single mistake: 'I'm useless.'
- After your boss snapped at you on only one occasion: 'She's horrible.'

You are not reaching a balanced conclusion by looking at *all the evidence* objectively.

Minimization: a tendency to discount any information that doesn't fit with your negative view of yourself or other people, e.g.

- After someone complimented you: 'He's just feeling sorry for me.'

Continued

- After your boss apologized for having snapped at you: 'She just wants something from me.'

You are not reaching a balanced conclusion by looking at *all the evidence* objectively.

Overgeneralization: when you arbitrarily conclude that a negative event will happen over and over again, e.g.

- After one unsuccessful job application: 'I'm never going to get a job.'
- After getting a flat tyre: 'This is just so typical: everything always goes wrong for me.'

You believe that there is a negative pattern that will continue, but when looking at all the relevant evidence, there is no sound basis for such a prediction.

Catastrophizing: dwelling on the negatives in a situation and believing things are worse than they actually are, e.g.

- 'My OCD has ruined my life.'
- After not getting the promotion: 'I'm a nothing.'

You may not be paying attention to aspects of the situation that contradict your negative conclusion (there may well be areas of your life that are relatively unaffected by OCD, and not getting the promotion is not the end of the world!).

Low frustration tolerance: persuading yourself that something is so bad that you absolutely can't tolerate it; this is frequently linked to catastrophizing, e.g.

- 'That he didn't give me the promotion is the most awful thing that could have happened' (catastrophizing); 'it's so unfair and I can't stand it' (low frustration tolerance)!

The reality is that your body and your mind can tolerate much worse. Better to tell yourself that it's not the worst thing in the world, that you can cope with it even though it may be unpleasant, and then deal with the situation calmly.

Inflexible demands: making rigid demands about things out

Continued

of your control (and then catastrophizing when your demand is not satisfied), e.g.

- 'He shouldn't have said that' (and the fact that he did is worse than terrible!).
- 'I must always win' (and if I didn't, that would be the absolute worst thing in the world and I couldn't bear it).

You cause yourself unnecessary upset by failing to recognize that not everything in the world is 100% under your control. Being upset does not help you to cope with the situation in the best way.

Emotional reasoning: when your emotions in or after a situation dictate your conclusion about yourself or the situation, e.g.

- 'I'm feeling anxious, therefore the situation must be dangerous.'
- 'I'm feeling embarrassed, therefore I must have made a fool of myself.'
- 'Unwanted thoughts make me feel anxious, therefore they must be dangerous.'

Your emotional reaction may have resulted from thoughts not reflecting the reality of the situation or experience; therefore basing your conclusion on your feelings only, leads you to a biased conclusion.

Negative prediction (or 'crystal ball gazing'): accepting your future predictions as fact, e.g.

- 'My OCD will never improve.'
- 'Treatment won't work, so what's the point of trying?'

The future is rarely 100% certain. Rather take action to help positive predictions come true!

Personalization: arbitrarily concluding that an event applies to you personally or 'taking things too personally', e.g.

- After your boss didn't smile when he walked past you: 'He's upset with me.'

Continued

You unreasonably exclude all other possible explanations for an event (e.g. maybe your boss is just having a bad day).

Mind reading: you assume that you know what others think, e.g.

- 'I got angry at him because I just knew what he was thinking!'

You may be wrong – best to check by asking or simply accepting that you can't be certain.

How CBT tackles emotional difficulties

In CBT, we learn to examine carefully our negative thoughts in situations. You may wonder whether this is all about changing negative to *positive* thinking? Sometimes yes, but not always. CBT is less about positive thinking than about *realistic* thinking. This is because we have to acknowledge that sometimes our negative perceptions of people, other situations or ourselves may turn out to be accurate. If we try to persuade ourselves to the contrary, we may end up becoming our own spin-doctor – unreasonably trying to force negatives into positives. At best, we may end up being over-optimistic or perhaps naïve. At worst, we may end up preventing ourselves from dealing with problems when this is called for.

How CBT makes sense of OCD

The framework I will be using is a variation of CBT theories of OCD, called the 'inference-based approach' (IBA), which was developed, by Professor Kieron O'Connor, Dr Frederick Aardema and Dr Marie-Claude Pélissier, in Montreal, Canada.

As previously discussed, the definitive symptoms of OCD are obsessions and rituals. But what is their relationship? On the whole, we know that obsessions *cause* anxiety or discomfort. In turn, ritualizing is then used to *reduce* the anxiety or discomfort caused by the obsession or to *avoid* the anxiety or discomfort that would result if the obsession were left unchecked. Therefore ritualizing inevitably represents a way of trying to reduce the unpleasant feelings stirred up by the obsession.

You may ask why the obsession causes us to feel anxious or uncomfortable, and what causes the obsession in the first place? To answer this question we have to think carefully about the nature of obsessions. They would almost always involve uncertainty about things being awry in one way or another – in that sense representing a doubt about things not being OK.

This obsessional doubt is where the OCD ball starts rolling; for example, 'the door looks locked … but perhaps …', or 'the object looks clean … but maybe …' or 'I know I don't need to walk through the door a second time ... but just possibly …' You may counter that when you experience an obsession, you're not simply uncertain about things not being OK, you're *certain* they're not. However, this only means that the doubt is so strong as almost to represent a sense of being certain, but in essence it still remains a doubt.

When you consider the possible consequences *if this doubt were true*, and you didn't set things right in some way, that usually represents a dangerous or unpleasant situation. For example, 'If the door is unlocked, my house could be burgled', or 'if the object is contaminated with germs, I could infect my child', or 'if I don't walk through the door a second time, something bad will happen'. It therefore makes sense to try and remedy the situation by acting on the doubt to make sure that the feared consequences won't occur. This can be achieved in a number of ways:

• performing a ritual to reassure yourself (e.g. checking the door a set number of times, despite knowing it is locked after the first check);

- asking someone else for reassurance (e.g. asking your partner if the door is locked after you have checked it yourself);
- avoiding the situation in future altogether (e.g. asking your partner to always lock the door).

To summarize, an obsessive thought always represents a doubt about things potentially not being OK (more guidance on identifying the doubt is provided in Chapter 5). If the doubt were true, and you didn't do anything to set things right, the consequences would be dangerous or unpleasant. Performing a ritual or asking someone else for reassurance represents an attempt to get certainty about things being OK. Avoidance of situations which trigger obsessive doubts is an attempt to sidestep the problem altogether. Unfortunately, these solutions do not deal with the problem of the obsessive doubts in any conclusive way and frequently only lead to more doubt. We will soon consider why this is the case. Figure 2 illustrates the relationship between the various components of your OCD (adapted from O'Connor et al., 2005).

How can CBT help my OCD?

The first part of Chapter 2 gave you an idea of the relationship between the obsessional doubt, what the doubt means to you, your emotional reaction to the doubt, and the strategies that you use to make the situation safe or reduce the unpleasant feelings caused by the doubt. Next we'll consider how to use this knowledge to tackle your OCD. First, we'll look at strategies that maintain your OCD and make it worse, and then we'll consider helpful alternatives.

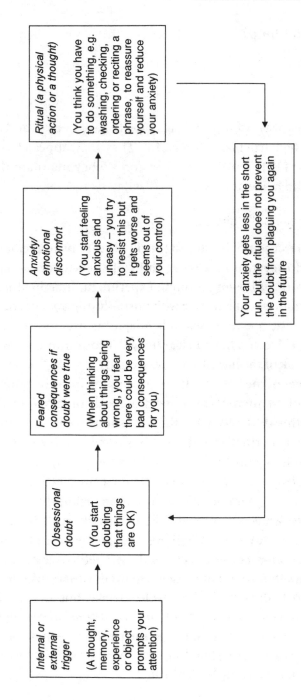

Figure 2 An IBA perspective on OCD

What doesn't help?

> Nothing fixes a thing so intensely in the memory as the wish to forget it.
>
> Montaigne

The following ways of responding to OCD have been found in research to be particularly unhelpful. They may appear to be helping your OCD, but in fact, they don't. They maintain the condition and make it worse.

Trying to suppress the obsessional doubt

It makes perfect sense to want to get rid of scary or unpleasant thoughts. However, this is more difficult than it seems. For example, try the following thought experiment: imagine finding a green fluorescent hamster with purple luminous eyes outside your house. Spend 30 seconds imagining exactly what he may look like. Do you have a clear image in your mind? Now – try *not* to think of the hamster for 60 seconds.

Did images of the hamster keep on popping into your mind despite your best attempts at suppressing it? People frequently experience this difficulty with thought suppression, and this may also apply particularly to the times when you try to push obsessions out of your mind. This is because obsessions, as we discussed above, cause anxiety and other negative feelings, and our brains are programmed to pay attention promptly to what we fear or to what puts our well-being at risk (ever tried to ignore a tiger while you were walking through the jungle?). This process sometimes becomes activated even before we are *consciously* aware that we are in danger. (In other situations it may protect us from danger and help us to survive, but as you will see, this is not relevant in OCD situations.) Therefore trying to push obsessions out of your mind by earmarking them *not to be attended to*, is a bit like switching the radar on and trying to ignore what it is bleeping back at you.

Ritualizing or reassurance-seeking

True, there is benefit to these strategies – you feel a bit better after you've performed your ritual or someone has reassured you, but this is usually only a temporary relief. Come the next situation where you experience the obsessional doubt, you have to repeat the rituals or find someone or something else to reassure you. The quest for peace and certainty by ritualizing is a gruelling journey, never completed.

OCD also has a nasty way of demanding more and more from you. Give it a finger and it takes the hand. As you give in to more ritualizing, you find yourself slowly slipping into a murky swamp where safety, contentedness and certainty seem to be ever further out of your reach.

Avoidance

It is understandable that you may be tempted to sidestep situations or objects that activate obsessions. The reasoning goes like this: no triggers – no obsessions – no problem. Unfortunately, this is a bit like the story where the patient complains to the doctor: 'My leg hurts when I walk,' and the doctor responds: 'OK, then don't walk'! By sidestepping situations that elicit obsessional thoughts, you may well avoid the unpleasantness of being harassed by them and having to perform time-consuming and frustrating rituals. However, this usually imposes limitations on your life and restricts your freedom and the choices you have.

But what if you don't really miss the activities that you've given up? Nevertheless, remember that there's always a risk that the OCD bully will start demanding *more* ritualizing and *more* avoidance, which may eventually add up to having a significant negative impact on your life. Also consider that avoidance tends to increase your reliance on other people for taking care of the activities you want to avoid. It reduces the flexibility you need when unforeseen events require you to perform activities which the OCD has put out of your range.

What helps?

We've established that thought suppression, doing a ritual to reassure yourself, seeking reassurance from others, and avoidance, help to keep OCD in business. Apparent relief is offered in the short run, but this 'advantage' is offset by the considerable long-term drawbacks, which allow the condition to become more entrenched. If these strategies work against us, what can we do to find a more durable long-term solution? CBT researchers came up with the following answers:

Address obstacles standing in the way of confronting your OCD, such as depression and low motivation

As we have seen before, low mood can sometimes trigger the onset of OCD or cause an exacerbation of existing symptoms. Various background influences may contribute to a tendency to feeling low, such as your attitude to life, the quality of your relationships, stress and an unhealthy lifestyle. Alternatively, the constant pestering by OCD symptoms and the limitations they impose may cause you to feel depressed and demoralized. Whichever way low mood develops, it tends to be associated with symptoms such as tiredness, sleeping difficulties, feeling disheartened and a sense of the future looking bleak. This leaves you in poor shape to tackle a formidable project such as dealing with your OCD, which can seem an inextricable part of your life. We will address these issues in Chapter 4.

Examine and change those thinking processes that feed into the obsessional doubt

You may point out that the obsessional thought simply pops into your mind – there is no 'reasoning' or 'thinking' behind it. This may seem to be the case, particularly if you've had the doubt in many situations, in which case it can start seeming automatic. However, if you examine the obsessional doubt carefully – rather than trying to suppress it, which we have seen is not helpful – it will become apparent that the doubt is always a *conclusion* about a state of affairs in the world. As with any conclusion we reach about things, there is always a chain of thought or reasoning leading to this conclusion, or an argument backing it up. For example, one part of the argument feeding into the doubt 'the iron may still be switched on' may be the following: 'I know that I checked a few times, but maybe I can't trust what I saw.'

Let's call this argument the '*OCD story*'. And it is the OCD story that gets you into trouble because it does not help you to resolve your doubt in the usual way, but actually only leads to more doubt. In Chapter 5 we will consider ways in which the OCD pulls the wool over your eyes by using the OCD story, which may seem deceptively logical and reasonable, but doesn't stand up to examination.

Examine and change your thinking about the negative consequences if the obsessional doubt were true

As illustrated in the examples above, the obsessive doubt holds a certain meaning for us. We have ideas as to which consequences are likely to follow if the doubt were true and we left the situation unchecked. In OCD, the consequences are usually pretty bad or scary and we may consider that we will be held solely responsible for such consequences. For example, if you left the iron switched on, your house may burn down causing you to be ruined financially, leaving you and your family destitute – all your fault.

Because the consequences are so negative – you may see a negative drama playing out vividly in your mind – it is very difficult to ignore the doubt. And so it is much easier to opt for playing safe by avoiding the situation altogether, or reassuring yourself by using a ritual or seeking reassurance from someone else.

However, if you were to examine your thoughts about the consequences if the doubt were true, you may discover that they are not quite as bad as you feared. For example, if your house burnt down your home insurance will pay out and you and your family will be very unlikely to become destitute.

This alternative viewpoint may allow you to be less upset or anxious when you have the doubt. Consequently, if you are less upset, it may well be easier not to feel that you have to do the rituals, or the urge may be less intense because you see less point in the rituals. Similarly, you may see less reason for avoiding situations that elicit obsessional doubts. Therefore there may be some scope for improving your OCD by examining whether the consequences would actually be quite as bad as you fear they may be if your doubt were true and you left the situation unchecked. We will be looking at this in detail in Chapter 6.

Nevertheless, we have to recognize that there are some circumstances in which your thinking about what may happen if the doubt were true, may be quite realistic – that is, those consequences may well be very unpleasant. In that case, this point is not as useful in working on your OCD, and it would be helpful to concentrate your efforts working in the areas listed previously as well as the one below.

Eliminate ritualizing, reassurance-seeking and avoidance

We have previously considered that performing a ritual or using other forms of reassurance-seeking in response to an obsession only helps briefly and then you are back to square one. A temporary reduction in anxiety or discomfort is achieved, but the anxiety is reignited the next time the obsession is experienced, and like a nagging mosquito, the obsession always returns! *Ritualizing is never a long-term solution.*

Why is this the case? The answer is to be found in considering the reasons for why you need the ritual in the first place. This may well be because you want to reduce your anxiety. But what is the origin of the anxiety?

The anxiety stems from the scary or upsetting consequences if the obsessional doubt were true. And you take these consequences seriously because you may think of the obsessional doubt ('something is not OK') as being *real or credible* – and so it all goes back to the doubt. Ritualizing may over time even reinforce a sense of the doubt being real and credible, as a consequence of repeatedly addressing the problem of the doubt as if it were in fact a normal doubt. For these reasons, doing rituals maintains your OCD.

The pitfalls of simple avoidance have been discussed previously. Similarly to ritualizing, consider that it only makes sense to avoid a situation that triggers obsessional doubts, if you consider such doubts to be valid. Ongoing avoidance restricts your freedom and also reinforces the doubt because you're acting as if the doubt were valid. Ritualizing, reassurance-seeking and avoidance will be addressed in Chapters 7 and 8.

Biological explanations and treatments of OCD

As discussed previously, certain ways of thinking set us up for developing OCD, and maintain the condition once it has started. These ways of thinking will be considered in more detail in Chapters 5 and 6. However, researchers have also uncovered evidence that biological factors may contribute to a vulnerability for getting OCD. When these combine with psychological factors, it may become very likely that you will develop OCD.

So which biological factors are involved? Studies using brain scanning technology suggest that people with OCD have patterns of brain activity that differ from those without a mental health condition, and from those suffering from different conditions to OCD.

More specifically, increased brain activity has been detected in regions of the brain, including the prefrontal cortex (at the front of the brain) and the striatum (in the middle of the brain). A researcher, Dr Jeffrey Schwartz, and his colleagues at the University of California Los Angeles (UCLA) believe that the prefrontal cortex produces warning signals and it is up to the striatum to switch the signal off. However, in the case of OCD, this process doesn't function as it should and the person may continue to have a sense of something being wrong because the danger signals aren't being switched off in the usual way (Schwartz, 1998). However, a tricky problem with this and other biological findings in OCD is whether the observed differences between people with and without OCD are a cause or a consequence of OCD.

Another theory holds that there may be a chemical imbalance in OCD. Most of the attention has been focused on a brain chemical called serotonin, given that drugs that change serotonin levels have been shown to be helpful in OCD (see below). Serotonin is one of a group of substances called neurotransmitters, which are substances that help with the transmission of nerve impulses in the brain.

The class of antidepressant drug that increases the effects of serotonin in the brain is called the selective serotonin reuptake inhibitors, or SSRIs. These drugs have been shown to reduce OCD symptoms in about 40–60% of people who completed a course of treatment. Examples of SSRIs include sertraline, paroxetine, fluoxetine, fluvoxamine, citalopram and escitalopram. (These are the generic names of the drugs – they are marketed under different brand names or proprietary names in different countries.)

The recently published National Institute for Clinical Excellence (NICE) guidelines in the UK, recommend that

SSRIs should be the medication tried first for OCD. Sometimes when treatment with an SSRI has not been helpful, treatment with clomipramine is considered. Clomipramine is a member of a class of drug called the tricyclic antidepressants, and it also affects the level of serotonin. Usually the tricyclic antidepressants are thought not to be helpful in OCD, but clomipramine is the exception. Dosing at the higher end of the dose range (i.e. the range within which a drug may safely be prescribed) is often required.

In the case of very severe OCD which does not benefit from treatment with SSRIs or clomipramine, an antipsychotic medication may be combined with a SSRI or clomipramine. Examples of antipsychotic medications used include quetiapine and risperidone.

Many people considering drug treatments for OCD are worried about becoming dependent on the medications. In this respect it may be reassuring that none of the treatments listed above are thought to be significantly dependency-forming (or habit-forming), so you will not develop a craving for the drug. However, drawbacks you need to consider include the following:

- Improvement in OCD symptoms in response to antidepressant medications is commonly delayed for up to 12 weeks after starting treatment. Mood symptoms tend to respond sooner, but this may also require a number of weeks.
- There is a moderate risk that OCD symptoms get worse again if you discontinue treatment with the antidepressant medication. Some studies suggest that more people relapse after discontinuing treatment with medication, and they relapse sooner, than after discontinuing behaviour (a forerunner of CBT with significant overlap) therapy.
- There is a range of potential side effects associated with medication; for example, in the case of the SSRIs you may

experience nausea, insomnia, sexual dysfunction or other symptoms, although most people tolerate the drugs with little or no difficulty. Initial side effects may wear off over time as your body adjusts to the medication. You may experience withdrawal symptoms after stopping the drug or when missing a dose; to minimize the risk of this happening your medical practitioner may advise you to reduce the dosage gradually. Always inform your medical practitioner if you experience unusual or persevering side effects or with-drawal effects.

But how do the biological theories and treatments square up with the psychological theories and treatments considered previously? You may well argue that both can't be true! The fact is that all of the theories we have considered, both psychological and biological, may provide us with accurate descriptions of a complex condition. For example, some research studies looked at the effects of CBT and drug therapy, respectively, on brain activity. Recall that abnormal patterns of brain activity have been found in OCD. Interestingly, successful treatment with *either form of treatment* led to some normalization of brain activity (e.g. Schwartz et al., 1996)! This shows us that different treatments can be beneficial, possibly by causing similar changes in the brain.

Which is more effective, treatment with antidepressants, behaviour therapy or CBT, or a combination of the two? At present the evidence points to behaviour therapy or CBT being equivalent to medication, but combination therapy may work better than either on its own. As said previously, there is a lower chance of symptoms recurring after finishing behaviour therapy or CBT, than after stopping medication.

Which is the treatment for me?

At this point you may well be pondering the question above – medication, CBT or both? Perhaps it may be informative to consider the NICE guidelines for the treatment of OCD that inform the National Health Service in the UK. They suggest the following: if your OCD causes only *mild* functional impairment (i.e. only little disruption to your daily life), brief CBT is the approach of choice. If there is *moderate* functional impairment, a longer course of CBT or a course of medication should be used, and if impairment is *severe*, a combination of treatments should be used.

Whichever you decide, CBT always has the potential to be useful. Medication may be helpful if: you do not make as much progress with the psychological approach as you would like to; if your OCD is severe; or if feeling depressed stands in the way of using CBT effectively (although CBT strategies can also be useful for dealing with low mood). You may consider the following advantages and disadvantages of CBT and medication when deciding which treatments to use (table 2).

Table 2 Advantages and disadvantages of cognitive-behavioural therapy (CBT) and medication

	Advantages	Disadvantages
CBT	Effective Small risk of relapse after end of treatment Also useful for treating low mood	Requires ongoing time and effort Time-consuming Expert help not always available
Medication	Effective Little time or effort required Also useful for treating low mood	Potential side effects or withdrawal symptoms Moderate risk of relapse after end of treatment

A cognitive track or behavioural track programme for overcoming your OCD

Chapters 1 and 2 provided a general introduction to OCD and introduced you to CBT. Chapter 3 will introduce you to eight people with OCD, whose progress we will be following in the rest of the book. In Chapter 4 we will consider ways of improving low mood and low motivation standing in the way of progress, and how to use self-help effectively.

Next, there are two treatment options to choose from: cognitive track treatment (Chapters 5–7); *or* behavioural track treatment (Chapter 8). Cognitive track treatment employs interventions aimed at changing the unhelpful *thinking* tendencies underlying OCD; in Chapter 5 the focus is on the argument supporting the obsessional doubt; Chapter 6 examines your thinking about what would happen if the doubt were true and you didn't do the ritual; and Chapter 7 concludes the work on the OCD thinking by helping you to reduce levels of ritualizing or reassurance-seeking in response to obsessions, or avoidance of situations that trigger obsessions.

The behavioural track option in Chapter 8 focuses on your rituals or avoidance more directly (i.e. on changing your *behaviour*). It uses exposure and response prevention therapy (ERP), a powerful treatment approach targeting ritualizing, reassurance-seeking and avoidance *directly*.

Moving on from direct treatment, Chapter 9 considers how to address your OCD in a holistic way, by also looking at the role of background factors, such as your attitude to life, your relationships and your lifestyle. Lastly, Chapter 10 focuses on how to prevent relapse and stay well. Figure 3 describes the focus areas of the various chapters in this book.

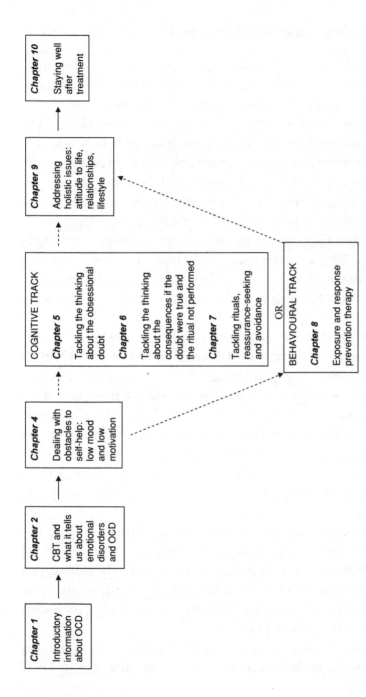

Figure 3 An outline of this book

Which programme is right for me?

As you will see in the following chapters, the cognitive track treatment option aims to reduce your anxiety by changing the thinking feeding into your obsessional fears *before* shifting the focus to the reduction of ritualizing and avoidance. The main approach in the behavioural track option is exposure and response prevention therapy (ERP), a forerunner to CBT approaches. ERP is a very direct and powerful therapy for OCD. It aims to reduce your anxiety by assisting you to systematically expose yourself to situations that trigger obsessions, and then reduce and ultimately eliminate performing rituals. People undergoing ERP find that their thinking about the situation changes and their anxiety gets less *after* they change their behaviours (i.e. face the situation and not perform rituals).

But which is the right option for you? To help you answer this, consider the situation in which your obsessions and rituals cause the most disruption in your life, or the situation in which your obsessions are the most intense. Ask yourself: what is my level of conviction on a 0–100% scale that something terrible will indeed happen in this situation *if I didn't perform a ritual or didn't avoid the situation*? If your belief level is *above 50%*, I recommend the cognitive track. However, if your belief level is *below and up to 50%*, the behavioural track may be appropriate for you.

Another consideration relates to the nature of your emotional experience in situations that trigger your obsessional fears. If the emotion is predominantly anxiety, the behavioural track may be effective; however, if your emotions are more complex, for example, also including guilt or shame, the cognitive track may be particularly useful.

An advantage of the cognitive track is that, in my opinion, it enables you to develop a better understanding of your OCD prior to reducing the ritual, and therefore allows a more insightful experience allowing you to stop the rituals in an easier way. Advantages of the behavioural track are that it is very powerful, generally less time-consuming and relatively more simple and straightforward than the cognitive track; however, anxiety levels and discomfort experienced during this programme tend to be higher.

My experience in my clinical practice is that the majority of people find that working on their OCD thinking benefits them through helping them to discover that their obsessional fears are unfounded or exaggerated and thereby making it easier not to ritualize or avoid. However, the two approaches are not mutually exclusive and the cognitive track also benefits from methods used in the behavioural track; for example, in Chapter 7 methods similar to ERP (in Chapter 8) are used to consolidate the work on OCD thinking described in Chapters 5 and 6. Ultimately you may prefer first to read the relevant chapters before making up your mind about which approach is the suitable one for you.

Key points

- Our thoughts in a situation influence our feelings and what we decide to do in response to the situation.
- Cognitive-behavioural therapy (CBT) aims to help you develop strategies for changing your thinking and behaviour in situations, to allow you to cope better.
- When applying the CBT model to OCD, we find that an obsessional doubt causes anxiety or other negative feelings. This is because you worry about what may happen if the doubt were true.
- You then do a ritual to set things straight or reduce the anxiety, or you ask someone else for reassurance, or you avoid the situation altogether.

- Trying to suppress the obsession, doing rituals or avoiding the situation maintains your OCD.
- Re-thinking the argument that supports the doubt and what you fear may happen if the doubt were true, and reducing ritualizing and avoidance, may help to improve your OCD.

PART TWO
HELPING YOURSELF

3

Meet eight people with OCD

In the previous chapter you have been introduced to the inference-based approach (IBA) model, which is a variation of CBT theories of OCD. This chapter will introduce you to Sonya, Andrew, Clare, Ahmed, Mark, Jenny, Sarah and Richard, who are struggling with OCD, and you will see how their problems can be understood within the IBA model.

Sonya

Sonya has obsessions about contamination by germs. She responds to her obsessions by performing rituals, involving thorough and lengthy cleaning. For about three years, since her daughter was born, she has started getting up increasingly early in the morning to clean the house before work, vacuuming every room and washing all the surfaces thoroughly. Currently she gets up every morning at 6 am, allowing her to clean for 90 minutes before work. When she gets back from work she cleans for an additional hour and then again for another half-hour after supper. She worries that her daughter may get contaminated with dangerous germs at the childcare centre, so she bathes her thoroughly in the evening and washes her clothes at the end of every day.

At work Sonya worries about using the staff toilet and her desk telephone, fearing that others may have contaminated the toilet and the phone. She thoroughly wipes the toilet with an antibacterial wipe before use and washes her hands for at least five minutes afterwards in scalding hot water. She checks her phone carefully and wipes it with an antibacterial wipe first thing in the morning and after being out of the office, fearing that someone else might have used it and contaminated it. She also washes her hands frequently during the day, just to make sure they stay clean. At home, she asks her partner, David, for reassurance about whether an object is really clean, despite knowing that she cleaned it thoroughly a few minutes earlier. They have stopped going out for day trips because she worries about using public facilities.

Outside obsessive situations, she calls herself 'bonkers' and mostly believes her fears to be unreasonable, although sometimes she is less certain of this. But usually the urge to clean is almost impossible to resist when she is feeling anxious. When asked what would happen if she didn't take precautions against contamination, she says that her biggest worry is that she might infect her daughter with germs, causing her to develop a dangerous illness. She would blame herself for not protecting her child.

Andrew

Andrew is unemployed and living with his father and his step-mother. He is pursuing part-time studies for a qualification in computer maintenance. Over the past year, after his step-mum moved in with him and his dad, he found that he was becoming insistent on items in his room and bathroom being ordered in a very specific way. For example, his bathroom towel has to hang exactly symmetrically. The rug in front of his bed has to be exactly square with the bed and, when he goes to bed, he makes sure that there are no folds in the rug.

When completing a college assignment he wants the typed pages to be spotless and without 'shoddy' wrinkles or creases before handing them in; frequently he throws away four or five pages before finding one that is 'just right'. He also finds that he is 'getting stuck' when switching off a light. He keeps on clicking the light switch until it makes just the right sound, before being able to move on to the next activity. When things are not 'in order' he feels restless and annoyed, and finds it difficult to sleep until things have been set right. Andrew doesn't really mind what the rest of the house looks like, even though his dad and step-mum are frequently not as neat as he would like them to be.

Clare

Clare lives in a semi-detached house with her two cats. She works as a legal secretary. Over the last few years she has started noticing that it is becoming more and more difficult to leave her house when going out in the morning for work, or when she has to do errands in town. She finds that she can't stop worrying about the possibility of having left the oven, iron or some other electrical appliance switched on. To reassure herself she checks all plugs and appliances twice to make sure that they are switched off before leaving the house. If there is an interruption in her checking routine, she has to start the full routine again to make sure that she doesn't miss anything.

Frequently after leaving the house she feels compelled to go back in to check again, fearing that she might have missed something or that her memory of previous checks was inaccurate. This has retrogressed to a point where she now needs to check for 20 minutes or more before feeling that she is able to leave the house. Sometimes, in addition to looking at the switch a number of times, she also has to touch the switch or feel the oven plate 'to make absolutely sure' that it is not switched on. Sometimes she feels that she has to assign a 'code word' to reassure herself that she did in fact check the switch. Despite being fed-up with the checking, she has been going out for social and other occasions less frequently than before.

When she is the last person to leave the office in the evening she follows a set routine for checking all the electrical appliances, being particularly concerned about her computer, and also has to start from scratch again if interrupted, perhaps by a phone call. She sometimes has to repeat the check, even if she wasn't interrupted, and finds herself staring at the computer button, having difficulty accepting that she has indeed switched it off.

Clare believes that her checking at home is excessive and unnecessary, and she is embarrassed about it. On one occasion a boyfriend was irritated when she repeatedly asked him for reassurance about whether appliances were definitely switched off. When he ended the relationship, apparently for other reasons, she wondered whether her checking might have contributed to the break-up. She now never invites men she dates home, fearing that potential partners may be put off by her checking, and think of her as being crazy.

She wonders if her problems might have had anything to do with an incident some years ago when a good friend's house burnt down, and the family dog died in the fire. Her friend was extremely upset and Clare had to calm her down. The cause of the fire was put down to faulty electrical wiring, but this was not established for certain. Clare remembered wondering if she may have contributed to causing the fire in some way, because she visited her friend the morning before the fire and had helped her cook breakfast.

Ahmed

Ahmed is married and has one adult child, a son, who moved to Australia. He now lives with his wife of 28 years. He is approaching retirement age but continues to work part-time as a caretaker for a local school. Over the years he has become increasingly fearful that when driving he may have hit a cyclist. It all started when he went over a large bump in the road one day, and suddenly had the thought that it could have been a person. He looked in his rear view mirror, but saw nothing. When he got home, he started feeling panicky, eventually driving back to the place where he went over the bump to check if there was anybody there. He didn't find anything, but wasn't reassured and later called the local police to hear if anything was reported, but they said that there had been no incidents.

Following this incident, Ahmed became increasingly anxious when hearing sounds or noises while driving, frequently retracing his route to check if he saw a body lying alongside the road. When passing a cyclist, he checks his mirror to confirm that the person is OK. He also checks the papers to see if anything has been reported. This means that driving causes him so much anxiety that he prefers to avoid it when he can. He never drives at night. He has similar fears and doubts when his wife is driving, but is prepared to accept her reassurance that nobody has been hit.

Mark

Mark was mildly worried after unexpectedly having a thought of pushing someone in front of an approaching train. He started taking notice of 'odd' thoughts and tried to put them out of his mind, but found this very difficult. He started having frequent thoughts about acting violently towards other people, particularly frail or vulnerable people, such as elderly people, pregnant mothers or children, including his own. He would see clearly in his mind's eye an image of lashing out in some unpredictable way, like punching them or stabbing them with a sharp object.

He regards these thoughts as highly alarming and very unusual, given that he thinks of himself as a family man – a kind and generous person, who places a high value on being helpful and considerate.

As a precaution against acting on these impulses he tries to avoid situations where he will be in close physical proximity to vulnerable people. When this is unavoidable, such as with his four-month-old baby, he makes a point of asking his wife to remove any objects like knives or metallic tools that could be 'used in an attack', and stands well away from the baby. He also changes aggressive images as part of his obsession allowing this to be 'cancelled out', such as imagining himself holding the baby instead of hurting it. This strategy allows him a brief respite until he is 'hit' by the next intrusive thought or image.

Jenny

Jenny is a mother in her early forties, divorced and now living with her new partner and two children – one from her first marriage. She took six months' maternity leave from her busy office job as an accountant after giving birth to her daughter. One day while she was bathing the baby she was very concerned when she glanced at her daughter's genitals and suddenly the word 'sex' crossed her mind. After lengthy reflection, she managed to reassure herself that there was nothing to it. However, she was alarmed again when she had the same thought the next time she bathed the child.

A few days later when she was changing for her dancing class she thought that a young teenage girl had an attractive body. This greatly upset her as she later wondered whether these thoughts might mean that she was actually a paedophile. She then started trying to look away from young people's bodies, and when she couldn't help but see them, she scanned her body afterwards for signs of sexual arousal. This led her to become conscious of many different sensations in her body of which she was previously unaware – although none of tell-tale sexual arousal. This led her to have even more doubt about whether she was sexually aroused or not.

She now pays even closer attention to her body and spends many hours of the day trying to reassure herself that she isn't a paedophile. When caring for her children, she tries to ban the word 'sex' or any word with a sexual connotation from her mind, but finds that she has great difficulty stopping herself thinking the 'bad words'. Sometimes the only way of being distracted is when something else goes wrong. She discussed the situation with her partner, who somewhat impatiently reassured her that he didn't think there was any basis for her fears. However, her doubts have continued, and she has become increasingly fearful and preoccupied about the possibility of being a paedophile.

Sarah

Sarah worked as an admin assistant in a busy office. She had been married to her husband, Sean, for less than one year when he became seriously ill while they were travelling in southern Europe. He developed a fever, dizziness and severe stomach cramps. The doctor wasn't sure what was wrong, but admitted him to the hospital and said he should rest while they kept an eye on him. Fortunately Sean recovered after a few days, but Sarah was very shaken, and at times during his illness it flashed through her mind that he could die. Following their return to England she kept on worrying about what might have caused his illness, and started feeling 'uneasy' about the risk of being infected. She did internet searches trying to help her pinpoint what might have caused his illness. But, what she found upset her even more. There were endless and confusing lists of symptoms, and all the viruses and bacteria and different kinds of 'bugs' she'd never heard of, that might cause them. She felt bewildered and worried that some of her own actions might have contributed to Sean's illness.

Sarah concluded that the only way of keeping herself and Sean safe was through prevention, not cure. Over and above her concern about infecting herself and others, she also worried about infecting her pet guinea-pigs with 'human germs', particularly the baby ones, to whom she was deeply attached. She started cleaning her house more and more thoroughly, scrubbing and using an old toothbrush to clean in the tiny nooks and crannies she would previously simply have ignored. She became increasingly worried about dropping items on 'dirty' floors, like in a public toilet. She became so anxious about using the toilet at work that she called in sick and stayed at home for a few days.

This was a crisis point, and her husband encouraged her to return to work, and try and cope by cleaning the toilet thoroughly before use. She eventually managed this, and succeeded in using the toilet by first thoroughly cleaning it, taking care not to touch any part of it with her bare hand, covering the seat with paper and then 'hovering' above the seat. Occasionally she couldn't avoid touching the toilet and this caused her considerable anxiety. She also became uneasy about touching other 'dirty' objects, like door knobs and office equipment, worrying that her colleagues might be sloppy, have dirty habits and not attend to their personal hygiene in the proper way. She appreciated that her fears were 'silly' and 'over the top', but found it hard not to yield to the rituals.

Richard

Richard has always seen himself as a careful and conscientious person – 'not someone who mucks about', as he likes to describe it. He has been praised for his careful work in the carpentry workshop where he does most of his work. He has always checked carefully that all is neat and tidy at the end of the day, and that the expensive equipment he used is locked away in a cupboard. However, recently at a time of some difficulties in his relationship with his wife, Marie, he found himself getting stuck on checking that cupboards, lockers and doors at work were in fact locked up, and whether windows were closed. He finds himself checking repeatedly, pulling door handles more than is necessary, staring at windows to make sure they are closed and standing on the side of the room to check that the windows and their handles are aligned in a way that would suggest that they are closed. He worries that there might be a burglary with disastrous consequences. His workmates have noticed his checking and have been teasing him about it, which was better in some ways than checking in secret, but which still embarrasses and shames him.

Richard's worries at work have spilled over to his home situation, and he becomes very worried every morning when leaving the house, and in the evening before going to bed, that everything is secure. When going to bed, he asks Marie for reassurance that everything is OK. Initially she would reassure him, but at some point started refusing when once was no longer enough and he needed to be reassured repeatedly. This caused him to be restless and upset, but they compromised that she would reassure him no more than once only.

He is thoroughly fed-up with his checking which he considers 'daft' and unnecessary, and wants to stop, also because it is a cause of frustration for Marie when they have to leave the house together. His checking has at times caused them to be late for appointments. She was particularly exasperated when once he broke a window handle because he pushed it down in such a forceful way, to make 'doubly sure' it was closed.

Another obsession which Richard is very embarrassed about and keeps secret from anybody else, even his wife, is that he would have 'bad thoughts' about their four-year-old, Sue. Sometimes when he thinks about Sue, or if she draws his attention, the phrase 'burn in hell' (or other words with a similar theme) would flash through his mind. When he becomes aware of this he has to manipulate the bad words in the obsession to form neutral words (e.g. 'hell' to 'shell'), and after that has to say a short prayer. He worries that something bad might happen to Sue – he can't exactly say what – if he doesn't perform his rituals. He tries as hard as he can not to think the bad thoughts, but finds that they keep popping into his mind at the most inopportune moments. Despite his vicar's reassurance that the thoughts have nothing to do with religion as such, he found the ritual hard to resist, though he occasionally succeeded, but not without some difficulty.

In the case studies below you will see some examples of how the IBA model applies to some of the obsessions experienced by the people you have met, and over Chapters 4–8 you will be following their progress with self-treating their symptoms. Previously we have distinguished the cognitive track and behavioural track treatment options. Sonya, Andrew, Clare, Ahmed, Mark and Jenny opted for cognitive track treatment (Chapters 5–7), and Sarah and Richard opted for behavioural track treatment (Chapter 8).

How the IBA model applies to our eight people with OCD

Sonya

Trigger: Has to use her office phone after she's been out of the office for lunch.

Obsessional doubt: Someone could have used it. It may be contaminated with dangerous germs.

Feared consequences if the doubt were true: I will be contaminated and infect my child who will develop a dangerous illness and I will be to blame.

Emotions: Anxiety.

Ritual: Asks her colleague and friend for reassurance that nobody used her phone. Checks the phone carefully for signs of dirt. Uses antibacterial wipes to clean the phone thoroughly, just in case.

Andrew

Trigger: Switches light off before bed.

Obsessional doubt: Maybe it didn't click in the right way.

Feared consequences if the doubt were true: I will lose control over my environment. If I stop trying before getting it right, I will be so upset that I won't be able to sleep. Prolonged sleeplessness is dangerous and can lead to a mental breakdown.

Emotions: Frustration/unease.

Ritual: Keeps on switching on and off until the switch clicks in the right way.

Clare

Trigger: Leaving the office in the evening after she carefully checked that her computer was switched off.

Obsessional doubt: I wonder if I missed something. The computer may still be on.

Feared consequences if the doubt were true: If it is left on, it will heat up and catch fire and the office building will burn down and someone may get hurt and all those important files and documents will be lost – and it will all be my fault. I will be sacked and end up jobless.

Emotions: Anxiety.

Ritual: 'Better to play safe' – goes back into the office and checks the computer and the windows once again.

Ahmed

Trigger: Driving.

Obsessional doubt: Maybe I hit a cyclist.

Feared consequences if the doubt were true: I will be arrested for a hit and run accident and sent to prison. I won't survive there. The tabloids will hound me – my photo will be all over the front page.

Emotions: Anxiety.

Ritual: Checks his mirror when passing a cyclist. Retraces his route to check for bodies or ambulances. Later checks the car for signs of a collision or specks of blood. Checks the newspaper for reports of a hit and run incident.

Mark

Trigger: His wife walks into the garden shed holding their baby; he is busy cleaning his garden shears.

Obsessional doubt: I may attack the baby with the shears. (He sees an image in his mind of doing it.) Maybe I'm dangerous.

Feared consequences if the doubt were true: I will destroy all that is precious to me. My wife will divorce me and I will be sent to prison for life. I won't be able to live with the guilt!

Emotions: Anxiety/guilt.

Ritual: Mark asks his wife to meet him in the house. He then visualizes holding the baby lovingly. He locks the shears away carefully before following her into the house.

Jenny

Trigger: Becomes aware that she noticed a young teenage girl's body.

Obsessional doubt: I may have wanted to look at her body. I may be sexually attracted to her. I may be a paedophile.

Feared consequences if the doubt were true: If this becomes known I'll be shunned and rejected by society. I'll turn into something sick and repulsive.

Emotions: Anxiety/guilt/shame.

Ritual: Scans her body for signs of sexual arousal for reassurance, but this creates a further doubt about whether she is sexually aroused.

Sarah

Trigger: Has to use a public toilet.

Obsessional doubt: It could be dirty – there could be harmful viruses or bacteria on it.

Feared consequences if the doubt were true: I could catch something serious and spread it to my husband and to my pet guinea-pigs.

Emotions: Anxiety.

Ritual: Cleans the seat with antibacterial wipes, taking care not to touch it with her bare hands; then covers it with toilet paper and suspends herself above the toilet while using it.

Richard

Trigger: Hears his daughter's voice in the background and has an involuntary thought about 'going to hell'.

Obsessional doubt: Something bad might happen to my daughter.

Feared consequences if the doubt were true: It's the worst thing I can think of. I'd be responsible.

Emotions: Anxiety/guilt.

Ritual: In his mind he manipulates 'hell' to become 'shell', and then says a short prayer.

4

Preparing for self-help

Great things are not done by impulse, but by a series of small
things brought together.

Vincent van Gogh

What are the preconditions for successful OCD self-treatment?
First, let us think about how motivated you are. The first part of
this chapter will consider ways in which CBT can help you build
your motivation and tackle low mood about having OCD, and
about life problems in general. Second, it has to be acknowledged that using self-help materials can present a challenge in
itself. You may sometimes feel discouraged, and reading about
OCD may sometimes leave you feeling anxious or embarrassed
about your condition. This is understandable, but to make
progress it is important that you and your self-help materials
work well as a team. The second part of the chapter will consider how to do this in the best way possible. The third part will
look at ways of making sure that you use all the help you can
reasonably expect to receive from family and friends.

Building and maintaining motivation

Being motivated means feeling ready to get on with the project at hand. Naturally, in the case of a big life project, such as facing a formidable opponent like OCD, this can easily seem daunting and overwhelming. You may be tempted to think that progress is impossible and that there is no point in trying. Or that this is 'just how you are', that you won't be able to change. Or you may think that progress is possible but may be very difficult and end up making a half-hearted attempt at improvement, expecting defeat. Or you may just find yourself procrastinating for other reasons – you've bought the book, it's lying on the table, but you just can't find the time to start reading it at the moment, there are more urgent things to do.

Let's examine more closely what your motivation about tackling your OCD depends on. In a nutshell:

- your thinking about the pros and cons of OCD (is it worth the effort?);
- your belief about your ability to improve your OCD (can I do it?);
- your ability to develop and implement your plan (What do I do? How do I do it? When do I start?).

This is illustrated in figure 4.

We'll consider each of these questions in turn.

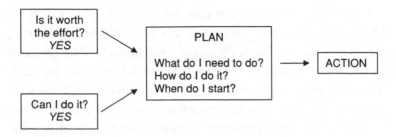

Figure 4 Motivation for tackling OCD

Is it worth it?

Try and write down the pros and cons of being rid of OCD on a sheet of paper. You may be surprised at being asked about the *pros* of OCD! It is important to recognize that a strategy frequently used by the OCD trickster is to make it seem as if the pros outweigh the cons. For example, even though you have less and less free time available because of all the rituals that you do and feel exhausted at the end of the day, OCD does pay you back by making sure that you stay safe, preventing bad things from happening and keeping the anxiety monster in its cage. These 'benefits' may start seeming more prominent as the condition becomes more entrenched and you increasingly structure your life on the basis of OCD thinking. As your life changes more and more to accommodate your OCD, different ways of thinking and acting become scarier – 'better the devil you know, than the devil you don't', as the saying goes.

However, consider the disadvantages carefully. Think about the impact of OCD on your work and career goals, your daily routine, your relationships and your hobbies and interests. Which valued activities have you stopped or started doing less frequently as a consequence of OCD? What have other people communicated to you about your OCD?

At this point you may recognize that the cons outweigh the pros, which justifies the problem being addressed without delay. If you're not convinced, think again carefully. The author's opinion – based on my professional experience, the experience of my colleagues, and hundreds of research studies – is that *OCD will never help you achieve your life goals.* It may appear to do so, but these benefits are illusions. If you disagree with this statement or if you are unsure about it, that's OK; the following sections will clarify this issue further.

Can I do it?

Rate your ability to make progress with your OCD on a 0–100% scale. Is your answer closer to 100% or closer to 0%? In the case of the latter, you may be feeling overwhelmed and hopeless about the situation, which may lead you to hesitate about trying to do something about it. You may hope that the OCD will improve on its own accord, without any active involvement from your side. Sadly, spontaneous improvement is frequently hoped for in vain, and a much more certain recipe for improvement is to intervene actively in the condition in ways that will be described in the remaining chapters. And active effort is not augmented by low confidence in your own ability to make a difference. So how do you boost your confidence?

A useful way of thinking about OCD is of a huge black mountain standing in your life path. You have to get over the mountain to get on with living your life in the way that you prefer. As you stand there looking at the mountain, you feel despondent. It seems ominously big and intimidating. What is to be done?

You carefully take a few steps closer, and realize that the mountain consists of rocks and stones! You move a few to the side of the road, and then a few more. You look at the mountain – no visible change. You feel demoralized and feel like walking away, but you carry on moving rocks, one by one. You start seeing a visible difference to the mountain. Your confidence grows and you keep doing the hard work, moving rocks, some big and heavy, others lighter and easier. Finally, you have moved all the debris to the side of the road, and can continue your life journey, a stronger and wiser person.

What is the moral of the story?

- Don't wait until you feel confident before you tackle your OCD project. This is putting the cart before the horse.

Greater confidence is the *end product* of tackling and mastering difficult tasks.

- A big blob of a problem can easily seem overwhelming, such as '*my OCD*'. Break the big problem down into many small separate problems, and start dealing with each in turn. In this way even big problems can be made manageable. For example, rate your ability on a scale of 0–100% of simply doing a pros and cons list of your OCD as suggested above. Your rating is probably quite a bit higher for this individual task than for your ability 'to make progress with the OCD'. You may well find that it is much easier to continue in this way, breaking big problems into smaller ones, and breaking major steps into minor ones.

What do I do? When do I do it? When do I start?

The remaining chapters in this book will give you clear guidelines for working on your OCD. So for now I will only offer the following general comments about the important topic of how to manage your self-help project in the most effective way.

Think of a person whom you would consider to be capable and productive. It may be the head of a big business, such as Richard Branson, or perhaps a friend or relative. What does their daily routine look like? You may agree that such a person is likely to be quite efficient at dealing with practical problems. In order to accomplish this they may require a great deal of *structure* in their life, such as a carefully planned daily schedule, dealing actively and promptly with problems that can be dealt with at the time, taking steps towards problem-solving other more complex problems and delegating tasks appropriately. The person's work environment would be well organized to make it possible to retrieve relevant information or materials easily. They may use an efficient system for recording important information on the go or reminding them to do certain things in the future, such as using a notebook, diary, email or phone. They won't procrastinate with important issues. They may strive for a balance between work and play, with time scheduled for relaxing activities or physical exercise.

Much may be learned from the habits and routines of very productive individuals – some of these are described above. You may retort that the people referred to above are facing practical work-related problems, not emotional or psychological ones. However, this is a false distinction. Dealing with emotional problems frequently benefits from a similar approach to dealing with practical problems encountered in your life. I suggest the following strategies for pursuing your OCD self-help project as efficiently as possible:

- Tidy your general living environment. A tidy environment generally benefits mood and assists in good problem-solving. (OK, there are exceptions to the rule – some people feel uncomfortable in very tidy environments! Try to find a balance.)
- Find a place and a folder for keeping your OCD self-help materials in an organized way.
- Buy a diary and use it (or use one on your computer). Schedule a starting date for your OCD self-help project. Also use your dairy for scheduling times in the week for working on your OCD. Tick items in your diary as you complete them. Remember not to expect panaceas, silver bullets or short cuts. This is a long-term project.
- Avoid procrastinating. Beware of the 'permission-giving thoughts' that give you a licence for avoiding or delaying OCD work for no good reason (e.g. 'I'm too busy right at the moment; I'll start when things slow down a bit' – when in fact there is ample time to be found and OCD is making a large contribution to a sense of 'being busy'). Think of ways of rewarding yourself appropriately when you have spent

time on your project. These rewards can be small and simple, like going for a walk, reading a magazine, watching a TV programme or making yourself a cup of tea.

The American psychologist, Dr Robert Leahy, emphasized that the decision to change should be less informed by what you *want* to do (we want to do many things!) and more informed by what you are *willing* to do. Be careful not to get bogged down on the former, and instead shift your focus to the latter.

Dealing with low mood

In Chapter 2 we considered the cognitive-behavioural model, which states that your thinking about events is important in influencing your mood and emotions. Negatively biased or distorted thinking (that is, thoughts which reflect on reality in an overly negative way) contributes to negative mood states.

Prolonged low mood, flatness or irritability may amount to clinical depression. In the case of depression, sufferers have recurring negative thoughts sometimes in the form of questions centred on some negative theme, for example, 'What caused my depression?' or 'Why can't I pull myself together?' or 'What does it mean about me that I'm depressed?' or 'Why can't I enjoy things?' Dwelling on these questions offers little reward and the person may find themselves sucked into a spiral of worsening mood, as this train of thought leads to one negative conclusion after another and their spirits sink deeper and deeper. (Psychologists refer to this kind of unproductive thinking as 'rumination', and this has been implicated as a powerful villain in explaining why some people are vulnerable to depression and why their depression persists. Ruminative thinking tends to occur at a general and abstract level, and is removed from helpful thinking centred on addressing specific problems directly.) Frequently, the negative thinking combines with negative behaviours in a potent depressive maelstrom by leading to an increase in 'depressant' behaviours (e.g. isolating yourself, 'self-medicating' with alcohol, staying in bed) and a reduction in 'antidepressant' behaviours (the activities you used to enjoy and made your life varied and interesting, e.g. exercising, seeing friends).

One challenge is how to respond to negative thoughts and behaviours and rumination when you are entangled in them already. A further challenge is how to prevent negative thoughts and emotion experienced over the course of everyday life from gaining depressive momentum. It makes sense to consider these questions separately for negative thinking and behaviours. A toolbox of three different strategies for improving your mood is outlined next.

Strategy 1. Answering and testing your negative thoughts

If negative thinking is the problem, changing your perspective to be more realistic and objective may alleviate emotional distress, depression or anxiety.

How is this accomplished? Easier said than done, because at the time you may be feeling miserable or anxious – mood states which do not help careful and objective reflection on your thoughts. It therefore makes sense to break the process down into a series of four steps which are outlined below (examples follow). (The 'Thought recording form', which you will find in Appendix 2 with instructions for completing it, will help you analyse your thoughts and feelings in situations according to steps 1–3.)

Step 1

Become aware of your thoughts and behaviour when you are upset or experiencing other negative feelings (identify your 'hot thoughts', which are linked to negative feelings, as opposed to 'cool thoughts', which calm you down). Ask yourself: 'What was going through my mind?'

Step 2

Learn to question your thinking and make it a habit (*remember: a negative thought should never simply be assumed to be a fact*). Consider two questions:

- Are my thoughts based on reality? Look at the examples of common thought distortions listed on page 21 in Chapter 2. Is there evidence of all-or-nothing thinking/magnification/minimization/overgeneralization/catastrophizing/low frustration tolerance/inflexible demands/emotional reasoning/crystal ball gazing/personalization/mind reading?
- Are my thoughts helping me to achieve my goals? If your thoughts are biased or distorted in a negative way, and provide an inaccurate description of reality, they are unlikely to be helpful to you.

Step 3

Formulate an alternative, more realistic, balanced and objective perspective on the situation. This may be a difficult feat to accomplish in the heat of the moment or when you are still very upset. It may be helpful to choose a calmer moment for this part of the exercise. Think of a calm and reasonable person you know, and think of how they would have viewed the situation. Or if you were having overly self-critical thoughts, think of a kinder or more generous perspective on yourself. Answer your negative thoughts with these alternative thoughts and imagine yourself being in the situation, thinking the alternative thoughts and acting consistently with the alternative view.

To further develop your realistic perspective on the situation, you may choose to do an 'experiment' to test your negative thinking, for example, trying out an activity to test your prediction that you won't enjoy it, or testing how people actually respond to you by looking them in the eye when you talk to them, instead of looking down at your feet. Before conducting the experiment, write down and be specific about which evidence would support either the negative view or the alternative view. Make sure you evaluate the results of the experiment fairly and objectively.

Step 4

After you have developed your skills in working on your negative thoughts in specific situations, it may be helpful to reflect on whether there are common themes or recurring patterns in your thoughts in diverse situations (what phrases would a parrot who could hear your thoughts be mimicking?). These may point towards pessimistic underlying beliefs or assumptions that you hold about yourself or other people, or unhelpful personal rules that you apply in an inflexible way. These may set you up to think in a negatively biased knee-jerk way in certain situations, without any convincing support from the situation for doing so. You may 'see' what you're (already) believing, instead of believing what you're seeing (objectively)! The negative belief may lead you to highlight experiences and information that fit the belief, and ignore what doesn't fit. In this way the belief may be maintained and even strengthened despite there being lots of evidence that doesn't support your negative conclusion.

Examples of negative self-beliefs include a view of the self as being fundamentally weak, vulnerable, helpless, incompetent, out of control, worthless, bad, unlovable or having bad luck or causing others to have bad luck. Examples of negative beliefs about other people include their being unable to fend for themselves, unreliable, out to exploit you or hostile. Following from these beliefs, examples of personal rules include, 'I must never make a mistake' (because if I do, my incompetence will be exposed), 'I must never take any risks' (because if I did, I won't be able to cope), or 'I must always look out for other people' (because they can't be trusted to look after themselves).

Ask yourself what the disadvantages are of living according to your personal rules? Perhaps having inflexible rules made sense in a previous time in your life, but is no longer justified by your circumstances and may no longer be in your interest. Does this present a case for changing your rule to a more flexible outlook? For example, it would have made sense not to trust anybody when previously in your life you were surrounded by exploitative people; however, this may no longer apply, and you may find that your new safer, social environment justifies opening up a bit more.

In respect of your negative beliefs, ask yourself whether reality really supports these negative viewpoints, and be careful to consider the evidence objectively. Relevant evidence may include situations or experiences in the remote past or in childhood, in which case you may want to consider whether at the time of having had the experience you may have been prone to negatively biased thinking, such as excessive self-blame. If so, try to answer these negative perceptions with realistic alternatives for that specific situation. For childhood experiences, ask yourself whether your perspective as an adult would be different to the child's perspective. If an experience was particularly powerful in influencing your thinking, it may be helpful to vividly imagine yourself being in the situation as a child; try and recount your upsetting thoughts and feelings at the time. You could imagine entering the situation as an adult, and reassuring the child with a kinder and more objective adult perspective. It may be helpful to write down all the past evidence inconsistent with your negative belief and formulate a fairer alternative belief that does justice to *all* the information, not just the negative information.

An alternative or complementary route to take is the 'belief under construction' approach. Ask yourself what kind of a person *you would like to be* and write this down on a piece of paper (e.g. 'I am useful', as the positive belief opposed to 'I am useless'). Monitor on an ongoing basis in an objective way the evidence in your day supporting the positive belief (e.g. when you do useful things like cooking dinner or giving someone directions in the street) and keep a daily record of the evidence. Or you could introduce actions into your day consistent with the new belief, building it up and strengthening it as you go along.

Sonya

In Chapter 3 you have noticed Sonya performing a ritual in her office of cleaning her telephone with an antiseptic wipe because she is unsure whether anybody else might have used her telephone without her knowledge. One day she notices a colleague talking to another and smiling when looking in her direction. Sonya feels embarrassed and blushes; she pretends that she is going to the toilet and leaves the room. You can see the thought recording form that Sonya completed for this situation at the end of this chapter (table 3).

After recording similar automatic thoughts in a number of social situations where she felt ashamed of others observing her rituals, Sonya decided that she may be holding an underlying belief about herself being mad and out of control, and that this was a shameful way to be.

After carefully considering the evidence for and against such a belief, she concluded that there was plenty of reason to believe herself to be a person with OCD, not *mad*, and thoroughly in control in many important areas in her life, such as in her work, managing the household budget and other areas. Sonya considered her thinking about other people with OCD and became aware of harsh double standards, where she was quite sympathetic and accepting towards others' limitations, but criticized herself severely. She continued this work by reflecting at the end of the day on evidence from the day that supported her new belief: 'I am coping and I am in control', and keeping a record of this evidence.

Andrew

> Andrew is keen to get a job. One day he is completing a job application form and gets to a section requesting details of his medical history. Andrew sighs, tears up the form and goes and lies on his bed, feeling low. See Andrew's thought-recording form at the end of this chapter (table 3).

Strategy 2. Getting active

As we have discussed previously, depression is frequently characterized by a downward spiral where low mood leads to you ceasing to do things you enjoyed previously, which in turn makes you feel worse, and so on (depression by nature tends to be a 'self-limiting' condition). Probably one of the most powerful strategies for reversing this trend is posed by simply getting active in a structured way. The experience of depressed people and the results of many research studies suggest that – contrary to your expectation when you are feeling low – increased activity will make you feel better, less tired, more motivated and with improved concentration. But getting busier is easier said than done. When people are depressed, every molecule in their body is crying out for disappearing underneath the duvet and staying there! The following two steps will help you along the way.

Step 1. Planning

Because your body and mind are pleading to do less, rather than more, you need the support of structure in your programme. One of the simplest ways of doing this is to get hold of your diary (buy one if you don't have one) and use it for scheduling activities that you would like to do more of (or use the calendar on your computer or simply a sheet of paper for planning the next day or week).

Make a list of activities that previously (before you started feeling low) you would have enjoyed or would have been useful to you. Try to find a balance between activities for enjoyment (e.g. hobbies, socializing, leisure activities) and problem-solving (e.g. opening mail, paying bills, work-related activities), and try to build in some reward if you manage to stick to your plan. Now, take your diary or planning sheet and pencil in activities for the next day, being specific about the time of day and duration of the activity. Keeping in mind your low mood and low energy, take care to be realistic about how much can be achieved. Generally it is advisable to follow a *graded* approach, where you gradually increase your activity levels over days and weeks. It also makes sense to do your planning of the next day at a time of day when you are feeling relatively more energetic (e.g. people with depression often feel more poorly early in the morning, although this is not a rule).

Step 2. Action

Try and stick to your plan and follow the schedule you have outlined in your diary or planning sheet. Tick activities as you complete them – this is likely to contribute to a sense of mastery and accomplishment. Be wary of the negative thoughts that can interfere with your progress and use the steps described above to answer them.

A short-cut approach to dealing with negative thoughts may also be useful when you find yourself thinking at length about whether you are motivated or whether you feel like doing the activity, or whether ... and so on. Cut short this counterproductive thinking and think of the Nike athletics company slogan: 'JUST DO IT', and follow suit!

Try to adopt an attitude of willingness to test out your negative predictions about what it would be like to perform the activity rather than accept them as fact. The important comparison is not whether you will enjoy the activity as much as you enjoyed it *before you got depressed*, but how it squares up to not doing it at all (e.g. instead sitting on the sofa or lying on your bed). If doing the activity provides even 1% more mastery or enjoyment than not doing it, this is still a strong argument in favour of getting busier, and will contribute to building the momentum for mood improvement.

Remember that the road to recovery is usually a rocky one, so expect that you won't always succeed in attaining your goals – this is where a flexible approach is required. Reflect on what didn't work out in a practical and specific way, problem-solve, work on the negative thoughts that impeded your progress and try again. Try to stop yourself from ruminating about not having succeeded and refocus on practical and specific strategies. Beware of unhelpful '*Why?*' questions, such as 'Why am I never succeeding?' or 'Why can't I snap out of this', and rather ask '*What?*' questions, such as 'What (specific helpful things) can I do now?'

Strategy 3. Cultivating mindfulness and acceptance

Mindfulness approaches involve the cultivation of an attitude of full awareness, attentiveness to, and non-judgemental acceptance of the present moment, which borrows from the practice of meditation in Eastern religious traditions. In my view it is particularly useful in offering an alternative to ruminative thinking, where the person unproductively analyses their problems and attempts to gain insight through dwelling on the discrepancy between things as they are and things as they should be, and ends up feeling worse as a consequence.

The abdominal breathing exercise described in Appendix 5 represents a simple strategy for engaging with a full awareness of one's breathing in the present moment. Ultimately, people who practise mindfulness cultivate an attitude of acceptance even towards their negative thoughts, choosing to allow them to enter consciousness and accepting their presence but not engaging with the thought in the way that characterizes dwelling and rumination. I like to think of it as being similar to standing on a balcony watching pedestrians walking by below, accepting their existence, not trying to control them, allowing them to enter the field of vision and amble along their way until finally they make their exit.

A full discussion of mindfulness approaches is not possible here, but if what has already been said is of interest to you, I recommend reading *The Mindful Way through Depression* (Mark Williams and colleagues, 2007), which provides a full discussion. Of course, mindfulness does not represent the only strategy for countering rumination. Distraction through engaging with a helpful activity, such as doing exercise, or directing thinking towards addressing concrete and specific problems offer helpful alternatives. The emphasis is on developing a repertoire of strategies, including all three discussed above, and using these flexibly according to the demands of the situation.

More detailed advice on using CBT to overcome negative thinking and beliefs, and alleviate low mood, may be found in the following books: *Mind over Mood* (Greenberger and Padesky, 1995) and *Reinventing Your Life* (Young and Klosko, 1998).

Enlisting the help of your partner, family or friends

In many studies on the effects of stress on well-being, good support by trusted others was associated with better coping and mood in the face of adversity. It is therefore important to consider the role of the important relationships in your life with respect to overcoming your OCD.

As we have established previously, when other people provide you with reassurance in response to your obsessions, often with the very best intentions, this may lead to a temporary reduction in anxiety – but this is always shortlived. They can provide reassurance in different ways: verbal reassurance that

something is OK when you ask them (e.g. repeatedly confirming that the toilet is clean or the iron switched off), performing
rituals such as checking or cleaning on your behalf, or
arranging the household or other routines in such a way as to
avoid situations that may trigger your obsessions. However,
reassurance by others in the face of obsessional doubt, in any
form, always perpetuates the problem. Learn to distinguish
reassurance that stands in your way, and reassurance that
builds you up, such as helping you to realize that there's more
to you than your OCD and that you *can* overcome it.

So how can you guide the people in your life to assist you in
the best way possible in helping you address your OCD? In the
following chapters you will explore different ways of thinking
about obsessional issues, which ultimately will lead you to feel
less need to obtain reassurance. However, to help you along the
way I suggest the following guidelines for enlisting the assistance and support of your family and friends:

- Educate the people close to you about OCD, in particular
  your spouse or partner if he or she is willing to be involved.
  Reading Chapters 1–3 may be useful for this purpose. They
  should recognize that ritualistic reassurance-giving is part
  of the problem, not the solution, and should preferably ultimately stop. Depending on whether you opt for cognitive
  track or behavioural track treatment, reading Chapters 5–7
  or Chapter 8, will also be helpful.
- Keep your partner up to date with your progress, and nego-
  tiate reductions in the unhelpful ways they try to help you,
  for example, by doing the checking, cleaning or other rituals
  for you (this issue is discussed in more detail in Chapter 7 for
  cognitive track treatment and in Chapter 8 for behavioural
  track treatment). Recognize that they may have busy lives
  and their own problems, and be sensitive to when it may not
  be appropriate to discuss your problems with them.

- If your partner needs your support, be willing to try to put your problems to one side and give your attention to them. Reciprocal support and nurturing are important to allow relationships to develop in a positive direction.
- Own up to your OCD problem and take responsibility for dealing with it in the best way possible. Don't blame your family.
- Some aspects of your programme may be more taxing than others. Think of which forms of support and encouragement would be most helpful to you, and educate trusted others about this. Be specific as to how you would like them to respond in difficult situations, for example, when you want to do your therapy work and they would prefer you to be going out with them.
- If you have friction with family members, refrain from over-general person-blaming statements (e.g. 'You never support me because you are selfish') and try to present the person with *a solvable problem* (e.g. 'When I wanted to ask your perspective on this OCD issue, you didn't have time; I really value your support – is there a better time for us to discuss this?'). Remember that providing a person with feedback on their specific behaviour in a specific situation in a respectful way is usually much more palatable to them than blaming them for having a global negative trait, like 'always being selfish'!

Key points

- Your motivation for your self-help project depends on your thinking about the pros and cons of your OCD, your belief about your ability to improve your OCD, and your ability to develop and implement your plan.
- OCD will never help you achieve your life goals.
- Waiting until you feel confident to tackle your OCD is putting the cart in front of the horse.

- Break big problems down into smaller ones and deal with each in turn. Reward yourself for completing each one.
- Big projects benefit from the right structure – structure your environment and daily routine in a way that helps your OCD project.
- Eliminate negatively biased thinking that causes unnecessary negative feelings – learn to question your thoughts and beliefs by weighing up the evidence supporting them.
- Enlist the support of your family and friends in a sensitive and effective way.

Table 3 Thought-recordings: Sonya and Andrew*

Date	Situation	Emotion/ feelings	Automatic thoughts (the 'hot thoughts')	Rational alternative perspective (the 'cool thoughts')
Sonya 20 Nov	I had just wiped off my telephone. Sandy looked in my direction, then smiled at Peter.	Embarrassed (80%); ashamed (60%) Blushed.	They are talking about my rituals and laughing because they think I'm stark raving bonkers. I can't stand this; I have to get out of here!	Sandy and Peter may or may not have smiled about me. I can't be certain of what they were thinking about at the time. Even if they did, that's OK, I can cope with having people occasionally laugh at me – it's not the worst thing in the world. Usually they respect me and we get on. I should focus my energies on overcoming my OCD and try not to be too sensitive to what other people think. OCD is just a mental health condition and nothing to be ashamed about; there is much, much more to me than my OCD. Embarrassment down by 30%; shame down by 50%.

Table 3 Thought-recordings: Sonya and Andrew* (cont.):

Date	Situation	Emotion/ feelings	Automatic thoughts (the 'hot thoughts')	Rational alternative perspective (the 'cool thoughts')
Andrew 7 July	Completing job application form. Got to the medical history section.	Low (80%), sad (85%), hopeless (90%)	What's the point? They'll never give me a job.	Yes, what *is* the point? The point is to do all I can to find a job. At the same time I'm working on my OCD. Doing nothing won't get me a job, the best that I can do is keep on trying to see what I can achieve. I can't be certain that they won't give me a job, that's crystal ball gazing. Nobody said getting a job was going to be easy, and this is the case for most people. There is legislation in place to protect me from being discriminated against because of my problems. I have previously managed to cope in a job despite obsessions and compulsions and got a reasonable reference. Low mood down by 30%, sadness by 30% and hopelessness by 50%.

* Please see Appendix 2 for instructions on how to complete the form.

A. COGNITIVE TRACK

5

Tackling the obsessional doubt

You can't depend on your eyes when your imagination is out of focus.

Mark Twain

In Chapter 2 we discussed the inference-based approach (IBA) model, which presents a cognitive-behavioural perspective on OCD. You may be able to remember that the obsessional chain starts with a prompt, which triggers an obsessional doubt. You may expect certain bad consequences to happen if the doubt was true, and therefore the doubt causes anxiety. You then use a ritual (or compulsion) to reduce the anxiety and this sequence repeats itself in similar situations. Or you may avoid the situation altogether. Take a moment to look again at the case studies at the end of Chapter 3, which provides examples of typical obsessional doubts. In Chapter 5, we will be working on the thinking underlying the obsessional doubt.

The difference between normal and obsessional doubts

In what way is an *obsessional* doubt different from a *normal* doubt? Consider the following situation: you come to a pedestrian crossing over a road; you think 'There could be a car approaching' (uncertainty and doubt). You listen – silence. You look left and right – not a car in sight (doubt resolved). You cross the road.

Now, carefully consider a recent situation in which you may have experienced an *obsessional* doubt. Did your ritual(s) resolve the doubt? Have you stopped believing what your senses (what you see, hear, smell, taste and touch) tell you or have told you, now and in the past, about the situation at hand? When outside the situation did your common sense tell you that the doubt was groundless and unreasonable? Did your doubt make trivial issues seem important?

Your answers to these questions are likely to point to important ways in which the obsessional doubt differs from a normal doubt:

- Normal doubt occurs in response to *direct* evidence from your senses and in *appropriate* situations.
- Normal doubt is resolved quickly once you get the proper information.
- Obsessional doubt occurs despite common sense telling you that all that is necessary has already been done.
- Obsessional doubt leads you away from the certainty of the information that your senses give you – this, and common sense, are no longer good enough.
- Obsessional doubt tends to get worse the more you think about it.
- With an obsessional doubt it is unclear what it is that will satisfy the doubt and give you complete peace of mind.

To illustrate the distinction better, let's consider the situation, described above, of the person getting to the pedestrian crossing. Notice how he used his senses (sight and hearing) to resolve the doubt ('Is there a car approaching?'), which occurs in an appropriate situation (pedestrian crossing), quickly and convincingly. He is clearly using a commonsensical approach to resolve a normal doubt.

But let's consider the situations, which activated Sonya, Clare and Andrew's obsessional doubts, described in the case studies at the end of Chapter 3. Sonya has the doubt that her phone may be contaminated with dangerous germs, which relies on the possibility that someone used her phone – but she has *no direct evidence* (i.e. from her senses) that anybody used her phone or that the phone is any different to how she left it. Similarly, Clare experiences the doubt that her computer may still be on, but has no direct evidence to suggest that this is a real possibility. In fact, the direct evidence (provided by her eyes at the time when she checked the computer) clearly points in the opposite direction. Andrew has the doubt that he didn't click the light switch in the right way (in response to the trigger of not hearing the click produce a crisp, satisfying sound). In this case the standard that he sets for the click goes against common sense, which would highlight the function of the click (switching the light on or off) rather than what it sounds like.

In summary, when trying to determine whether a doubt is obsessional, ask yourself the following questions (a 'no' answer to the first four questions and a 'yes' to the last two questions would suggest that the doubt is obsessional):

- Does the doubt occur in response to direct evidence or information and in an appropriate context?
- Is the doubt resolved quickly and easily once the appropriate information is obtained?
- Is the doubt commonsensical?

- Do you know precisely what you are looking for when you doubt?
- Does the doubt go beyond the certainty of what your senses tell you?
- Does the doubt become more difficult to dismiss as you think more about it?

Why is the obsessional doubt so strong?

At this point you may have a better sense of the ways in which your obsessional doubts are different from normal doubts. But why is the obsessional doubt so powerful and so difficult to dismiss? (One person described the doubt as attaching itself to you with a bit of gooey elastic, which keeps on pulling you back no matter how hard you pull against it!)

The answer to this question lies in the fact that the doubt is a *conclusion*, and as with all conclusions, relies on an *argument* to support it. And, in the case of OCD, this argument may *appear* to be very strong. It is possible that you may not be immediately aware of a line of thought feeding into your doubt, and it may seem as if the doubt lacks a supporting argument, but this may simply suggest that you have lost sight of the argument along the way. This is to be expected if you have experienced the obsessions for a long period of time. In that case, after a while the obsessional pattern may become quite automatic as you spend less time thinking about the obsessional doubt, and simply responding as if the doubt were valid or true. It's a bit like learning to drive – in the initial stages you thought carefully about what each traffic signal meant or about the mechanism of changing gear, but after a while you just perform the required action without giving it much conscious thought.

But how do we identify the argument underlying the doubt? The following questions may help you to do this when you have a specific doubt in a specific situation: 'Why may this doubt be true?' or 'Why is it possible that this doubt is true?' According to the IBA approach it may be helpful to think of whether your OCD story relies on any of the following sources: common knowledge, authority, hearsay, previous experience and logical calculation. For example, Sonya came up with the following OCD story supporting the doubt about her phone being contaminated with germs: germs exist – they cause illness by infecting people and may be transmitted by touch (*common knowledge*); my GP said that keeping things clean helps to prevent infection (*authority*); I heard of someone catching something from using a public phone (*hearsay*); I once got ill after my flatmate got a cold (*previous experience*); and there is always a possibility of infection (*logical calculation*).

You may respond to the above by pointing out that you don't, in fact, believe your obsessional doubts very much. This is to be expected for some people, as the level of belief in the doubt tends to vary between different people and different situations. (A common experience is that the doubt is stronger in the actual situations in which it is triggered than when reflecting on those situations from a distance, and is stronger when you are feeling anxious or stressed.) However, even if your belief in the doubt is low, this does not mean that following the steps described below wouldn't be useful for your OCD. I believe that it is always helpful to examine carefully your obsessional doubts, as they feature in a range of situations, to understand them better and to reduce even relatively low levels of belief in them even further. You may, additionally, benefit from the work on your thinking about the feared consequences if the doubt were true, described in Chapter 6, and the work on eliminating ritualizing, described in Chapter 7. Also be careful about being fooled into thinking that you don't actually believe the doubt, by saying that you know it's not true, but you can't take the chance that it isn't (and that's why you have to perform the ritual). This implies that you believe the doubt to the extent of having to perform the ritual, and therefore it still makes sense to examine whether there is a sound reason for believing the doubt. If there isn't any reason at all, you may be fooled into believing that you don't have any control over performing the ritual, which is just a further extension of the OCD con game.

In summary, the obsessional doubt relies on an argument for why it is real or why it should be taken seriously. The argument may appear to be strong, but there are important flaws in it, which we will be looking at next.

The argument (or 'OCD story') supporting the doubt

> But man – let me offer you a definition – is the story-telling animal.
>
> *Waterland* (Graham Swift)

This 'story' is the handiwork of a crafty conman, and, like any conman, OCD has a number of tricks up his sleeve to get you to take the doubt seriously. In the list below, you can see how he does it. Furthermore, your OCD story may also use any of the thought distortions previously discussed in Chapter 2 (see list on page 21), either in combination with the OCD thinking devices listed below or contained in them, to get you sucked ever deeper into the quicksand of doubt.

If you look carefully at the list of thinking devices it may become apparent to you that they all achieve the same goal: *they lead you away from reality and common sense into the shadowland of OCD.* In 'OCD-land' you start taking scary or discomfiting possibilities seriously. A very remote *possibility* – of which an infinite number exists – may be made to seem *very probable.* These possibilities are not supported by any direct evidence in reality or common sense. And if their origin is not in reality, then they can only be coming from the imagination.

This is not to argue in a critical way, that your 'fears are all imagined'. We have to recognize that the human imagination is an important faculty, which is put to use in many productive ways. Think of all the great works of art and literature that have been produced by the human imagination over centuries. However, in the case of OCD, the imagination is put to use in a *counterproductive* way in the wrong setting. The obsessional doubts cause needless anxiety and discomfort, and lead you to work overtime without any meaningful return. That is because, with their origins in the imagination, they will only stand in your way in coping with the demands of the real world.

How does an imaginary argument become so persuasive? One reason is the use of the OCD thinking devices. Another lies in why a good novel or a good film is compelling (think of how your heart races when the policeman tracing the killer's telephone call tells the lone woman in the dark house that the call is coming from *inside* the house ...). Both rely on suspense, a convincing storyline and a clever plot. In a similar way the imagination provides a compelling storyline in the shape of the argument supporting the obsessional doubt. It may be a well-developed story, which links together elements of the past and the present in your life experience. On the face of it the pieces seem to fit, making it seductively easy to believe and think of as being important; hence calling the argument underlying the obsessional doubt the '*OCD story*'.

As you repeatedly mull over the scary possibilities contained in the OCD story and act consistently with the obsessional doubt (by performing rituals or avoiding the situation), this rehearsal reinforces the sense of the doubt being imminent and real. What started as one of an infinite number of remote theoretical possibilities has evolved in your mind to become a real and likely probability.

To illustrate the above, it may be helpful to do a small exercise. As you're reading this you may be sitting in a room in your flat or house. You do not doubt that the roof is going to fall in, because, if you did, you wouldn't be sitting reading! If you considered such a doubt, it would be easy to dismiss – you don't see any cracks appearing in the roof, you don't hear the sound of cracking mortar, you don't see and hear falling bricks, and so on. You trust your senses.

Now, try to create an OCD story for why this doubt should be treated as real. You may come up with the following: I read in the paper about a building roof that caved in and people were injured, so this roof could cave in (confusing the link between events – this was an event separated in time and place from where you find yourself now); I've heard that some building contractors are corrupt and don't use the proper materials, so the person who built my house could have done the same (confusing the links between people – there is no evidence that the builder of your building did this); there may be some silent cracks appearing in the roof which I can't hear or see (creating imaginary stor-ies), so the roof could suddenly crash down, and so on. I think you get the idea – this is how an OCD story can be constructed from the imagination to support the doubt that 'maybe the roof is going to collapse', despite what your senses tell you.

OCD thinking devices

Making unsupported links between objects or items*

Linking items or objects as if one has something to do with the other, e.g.

- 'If that table is dirty, then this one must be dirty and needs cleaning' – despite the table looking clean (not recognizing that they are separate tables – the one may well be dirty and the other clean).

* Note that examples may sometimes be correctly classified as more than one thinking device.

Making unsupported links between events

Linking events, separated by time and space, as if one has something to do with the other, e.g.

- 'My friend often forgets to lock his door, so mine could be unlocked' (the two of you are separate people living separate lives – whether he locks his door, or not, has nothing to do with you).
- 'I read in the newspaper about a woman who swallowed a piece of glass in her food, so there could be glass in my food' (she is a separate person and this was a separate event).

Making unsupported links between people

Linking people as if one has something to do with the other, e.g.

- 'People have done terrible things, like commiting murders, so I may do something terrible' (this makes a confusing link between you and people who murder, going against what you know about yourself in reality).

Making unsupported links between experiences, thoughts or actions

Linking different experiences, thoughts or actions as if one has something to do with the other, e.g.

- 'If I can't control my anxiety, I also won't be able to stop myself from doing what I am thinking of, like when I have the thought of pushing someone in front of the train' (this involves confusing the experience of anxiety with unwanted aggressive acts, and confusing *having a thought* with *doing something* – despite there being no *intention* to act on the thought and no evidence from reality suggesting you are unable to stop yourself from acting aggressively if you didn't want to! The latter was called *thought – action fusion* by a Canadian researcher, Professor Jack Rachman).

- 'Thinking something is as bad as doing it' (this is a further example of confusing *thinking* with *doing*; also keep in mind that the goodness or badness of a thought is also determined by the intention to act on the thought – is there any direct basis in reality that you intend to act on the thought?).

- 'People can go into trances, so when I was sleepy I might have gone into a trance and done something without knowing I did it' (being sleepy is not the same as being in a trance, and there is no direct evidence that you were in a trance).

- 'I sometimes can't remember things, so that means I can't trust my memory about whether I attacked someone' (this involves confusing the experience of forgetting *minor* events with forgetting *major* events; is there any evidence in reality that you would forget a major life changing event, such as attacking someone?).

- 'I'm terrified about having thoughts about being sexually attracted to animals, which means that I must be attracted to them' (this confuses thinking about the *possibility of having an unwanted thought* with *engaging in*

Getting caught up in thinking about thinking ...

desired thoughts – having thoughts about the unwanted possibility of being sexually attracted to animals is not the same as fantasizing about them sexually).

Making unsupported links between thoughts/actions and events

Linking a thought/action and an event as if one caused the other, in the absence of support for such a link from any convincing source, e.g.

- 'One day I had angry thoughts about my friend and the next day I heard they had an accident so the thoughts might have caused the accident' (this involves confusing the link between a thought and an event – there is no basis in reality that thinking about an external event can make it happen; just think about all those people dreaming about winning the national lottery every weekend!).
- 'One day I lied to my father, and the next day he heard that he had cancer, so my lying could have caused him to get ill' (this involves confusing the link between an action and an event – without any basis in reality and without any support for such a link from any convincing source).

Making unsupported links between settings

Linking settings as if one has something to do with the other, e.g.

- 'Operating theatres are sterilized every time to protect the patients from the blood and germs. So if my friend's hand bled on my table, her blood must be dangerous, and the table has been contaminated and has to be thoroughly sterilized' (your home is not an operating theatre and your friend is not a patient! There is also an unsupported link between people, because you're not a patient undergoing surgery and therefore you are not vulnerable to infection in a similar way).

Introducing secondary doubts with no evidence from the situation

Secondary doubts (i.e. further doubts in the OCD story feeding into the initial doubt) are introduced from the imagination without any direct evidence in the situation to justify this, e.g.

- 'Maybe the door is unlocked because there could be a problem with the lock' (the lock was working fine yesterday; there is no immediate evidence from reality to suspect that it will not be working today).
- 'The door handle could be contaminated because the hospital is just down the road and a patient with a serious condition could have touched the handle and contaminated it' (there is no direct evidence from the situation that a patient with a serious infectious condition touched the door).

Wheeling in facts inappropriately

Facts are inappropriately applied to personal situations (i.e. without there being direct evidence in the situation to justify this), e.g.

- 'Germs exist, so there could be germs infecting my hand' (germs do exist, but there is no direct evidence that there are dangerous germs on your hand, e.g. you haven't shaken hands with a person with flu).

Creating imaginary stories

Telling imaginary stories without any basis in reality and not coming from a convincing source, e.g.

- 'I can imagine the microwaves entering my skin and damaging the underlying tissue' (without any evidence in reality).

- 'Three is my lucky number because I was born on the third of March, so if I do everything in threes bad events will be avoided' (without any basis in reality and a lack of support for such a link from any convincing source).

Reaching upside-down conclusions

Conclusions about reality are reached before, rather than following observation of reality, e.g.

- 'Many people must have walked over this carpet, so it must be dirty' (even though the carpet looks clean).
- 'Dangerous chemicals are used everywhere, so there could be some on my hand' (without any direct evidence that this is the case, e.g. you haven't recently handled dangerous chemicals for a domestic purpose without cleaning your hands afterwards).

Distrusting your senses

Not believing what your senses tell you, without a convincing reason, based on reality, for doing so, e.g.

- 'Even though the object seems clean, my intellect tells me that it is not'.
- 'Even though I saw the switch being turned off, maybe I

What your senses tell you is no longer good enough

"Just checking that I've turned off the lights, dear!"

didn't look carefully enough' (there is no good reason to distrust what your senses tell you).

Creating arbitrary or exaggerated standards

You create an arbitrary or exaggerated standard for objects, activities or thoughts, which has no commonsensical relation to them. Frequently such standards would emphasize other qualities at the expense of function, e.g.

- 'My DVD covers must not have any dust on them' (whether they have dust on them is irrelevant for what they have to do – label and protect the DVD).
- 'When I click the light switch, it has to click in the right way by making the right sound' (how it clicks has no relation to what it is meant to do, i.e. switch the light on or off).
- 'My toothbrush has to be exactly parallel to the wall' (the *exact* position of the toothbrush to the wall has no relation to whether it is easily found when needed).
- 'When I visualize my friend's face, the image has to be just right … in a way that is difficult to describe, before I can allow myself to stop thinking about it' (demanding this indefinable standard to be achieved has no commonsensical function. Also, you may find yourself chasing after the pot of gold at the end of the rainbow because it is so difficult to know exactly at which point your goal has been achieved!).

Making unrealistic demands about being able to control your thoughts or about the kinds of thoughts you have

Making demands of your brain that cannot be met, e.g.

- 'If I can't stop a thought entering my mind, this means that I'm losing control' (it is impossible to control *all* your mental activity because a large part of your thinking happens automatically – trying to block a disturbing thought

completely from intruding into your consciousness is impossible for anyone and may result in your being pestered by the thought. This is normal and not the same as losing control of *all* one's abilities, or going insane).

- 'If I can't stop an unwanted violent/sexual thought entering my mind, this means that I must want to act on it' (this is a special case of making an unsupported link between an experience and a thought, i.e. not being able to control the thought = wanting to act on it, while there is no evidence from reality that you have an *intention* to act on the thought. Instead, the evidence from reality suggests that you hold a scary obsessional doubt about yourself, with no basis in reality or common sense, which makes it difficult/ impossible to ignore the thoughts or block them from entering your mind).

- 'I had this odd thought in church about saying something really rude; this must mean there is something wrong with me' (most people have the occasional odd or inappropriate thought – this is a sign of how creatively our brains work and not a sign of abnormality).

Making unrealistic demands about feeling confident about your memory

This applies to repeated checking, where you unrealistically demand feeling confident about what you remember about having checked. It can apply to the checking of physical objects or situations or 'checking' your own memories, e.g.

- 'I know that I've checked the windows and the door many times, but I just don't feel confident that I did' (your reduction in confidence is a normal consequence of repeated checking and anxiety, which encourage a sense of uncertainty about what you saw or if you checked. A Canadian researcher, Professor Adam

Radomsky, has shown that this is also experienced by people without OCD when they do lots of checking and it says nothing about the accuracy of what you remember, which stays the same whether you check once or ten times! Memory confidence starts suffering as soon as you check *more than once only*).

- 'I've gone over the image in my head of locking the door many times, but still don't feel confident that it is locked' (your memory confidence is likely to get less as you 'check' the memory more and more).

Emotional reasoning

This happens when you think that the doubt is true because of how you feel when you don't perform the ritual, in the absence of any other convincing reason, e.g.

- 'I didn't perform the action in the right way by doing it once only, because if I just left it – that is, not repeat it in multiples of three – I'd feel extremely anxious afterwards and not be able to sleep' (whether the activity was performed in the right way should be determined on the basis of common sense, not solely on the basis of your feelings if you didn't perform the ritual; in fact, the anxiety will eventually get less if you *didn't* perform the ritual – see Chapter 7. This is quite a clever con because you first take it that your anxiety means the doubt is true, and when you believe the doubt is true you feel anxious when you don't perform the ritual, and this anxiety in turn provides further 'proof' that the doubt is true, and so on. This is a case of a dog chasing its own tail, or a *circular argument*).

The selectiveness of the obsessional doubt

One striking fact about OCD is how obsessional doubts feature in *selective* areas in a person's life. Out of an infinite number of possibilities for how things could be awry in one way or another, your OCD thinking latches on to only one or only a few possibilities to be taken seriously. For example, Sonya is concerned about germs transmitted by physical touch, but not by breathing. Andrew has doubts about his bedroom light switches, but not about switches for other electrical appliances. Clare has obsessional doubts about whether she switched *off* electrical appliances in her house, but is confident that she switched them *on*.

Not only do you think in most situations in your life in a way that does *not* produce obsessional doubt, but also frequently, before the OCD started, your thinking in the obsessional situations might have been quite different. At such a time, you might have trusted and been content with what your senses told you, relied on your common sense and not created imaginary stories.

To summarize, the obsessional style of thinking applies to selective areas of your life, and you may not always have been thinking in this way. This is good news for your project to overcome your OCD because this suggests that you already have intimate knowledge of ways of thinking that do not produce obsessions.

Why do I have obsessional doubts about certain issues?

You may well wonder why you experience these obsessional doubts in such selective areas of your life? One part of the answer is that you may lack confidence in yourself in some areas – as we all do – or hold a negative prejudice about yourself. These areas of low confidence or negative prejudice may reflect the beliefs you developed about yourself and the world as a consequence of your past experiences, including your childhood. However, if a thinking tendency that leads you to question reality and common sense latches on to an area of low confidence, this may lead you to be vulnerable to obsessional doubts and OCD.

One way of identifying such an area of low self-confidence or negative prejudice is to think carefully about your obsessional doubt. For example, if your doubt relates to a fear of touching a contaminated object and infecting others with a serious illness, you may think of yourself as someone who may be careless and make dangerous mistakes. If your doubt concerns potentially attacking someone else, you may think of yourself as someone who may be violent and dangerous. Or if your doubt is about having inappropriate sexual impulses, you may think of yourself as someone who may be perverse and sexually abnormal.

The steps described below aim to help you come to terms again with what reality tells you in obsessive situations, and address the OCD story that supports the doubt. By working in this way on your obsessional doubts in individual situations, you will also slowly restore your self-confidence in the areas in your life where you have lost faith in yourself.

Answering the OCD story

Picture a courtroom with the prosecuting attorney making a seemingly powerful argument trying to get the jury to accept what he knows is a very biased version of events. When the time comes for the defence to present their case, there's only silence. It turns out that the attorney for the defence, despite having a strong case based on objective facts, was not prepared for the points made by the prosecution, and therefore could only respond in this very feeble way.

Who will the jury believe? Of course, the prosecuting attorney will win. The point is that a clever argument, albeit a false one, will win the day if it goes unanswered and unopposed with a good argument!

In the same shrewd way OCD may seem to be making a compelling case, albeit on an imaginary basis, which has been winning the day. This presents the challenge to you of developing an alternative account to the OCD story for each of your obsessional doubts, an alternative account which avoids the thinking errors listed above, and consolidates with what reality and common sense tell you.

Formulating such an alternative account – and eventually acting consistently with it, *that is, not avoiding the situation and not doing the ritual* – offers you the following advantages:

- Allowing you to act in your own interest and the interest of loved ones by freeing up time and energy to deal vigorously with the real and visible problems and dangers in life, and not being held hostage by select remote possibilities or non-commonsensical dilemmas.
- Treating the obsessional situation(s) no differently to how you treat other situations in your life; that is, dealing responsibly with realistic problems if and when they arise and taking appropriate precautions where there is a commonsensical reason to do so.
- Not being held back by the OCD conman stealing your time, energy, money and freedom.
- Dealing with the situation or issue in the way that society expects of a reasonable and sensible person.

Below I outline a five-step plan for working on the OCD story feeding into your obsessional doubt.

Step 1. Identify the obsessional doubts and the situations in which you have them

Make a list of important situations in your life in which you experience obsessional doubts. You may find that the same doubt features in different situations (e.g. that the front door at home may be unlocked, as well as the door at the office, and the car door) and this may be the main problem. Or you may find that different doubts occur in different situations (e.g. that the mail delivered to your door may be contaminated or that the iron may be left on). It doesn't matter if you haven't listed every single situation for every doubt – try to be comprehensive, but what matters more is to get the most important ones down on paper; for example, doubts you encounter frequently or that cause you a great deal of distress.

For each trigger situation, describe the obsessional doubt, the expected feared consequences if the doubt was true, and the ritual performed to reduce anxiety and unease.

To help you identify the *doubt* (and any linked negative meanings), ask yourself: '*What do I think is not OK in the situation?*' and '*What is it I have to be 100% sure of not to have to perform the ritual?*' Here are some examples:

- There could be dangerous germs on the door handle.
- Maybe the envelope has a repulsive substance on it.
- Maybe the substance is blood (when you see a red spot) – maybe the blood is HIV-positive.
- Perhaps the iron has been left on.
- Maybe uneven numbers are unlucky.
- Maybe I'll miss something (if I don't follow the steps precisely).
- Maybe the t-shirt will be in the wrong place (if it is not arranged with t-shirts of the same colour).
- There could be a scratch on my DVD cover – my DVD could be spoiled.
- I could become an evil person (if I think a blasphemous thought).
- Maybe I'm dangerous – I could attack someone impulsively against my will.
- Maybe I'm sexually abnormal – I could be sexually attracted to a family member.
- I might have made a serious mistake.

- Perhaps I'll need this item in the future, even though I don't see any use for it in the present.

To help you identify the *feared consequences* if the doubt were true, ask yourself: '*What do I worry may happen if I didn't do the ritual and the doubt were true?*' or '*Which events may follow if I didn't do the ritual and the doubt were true?*'

To help you identify the *ritual*, ask yourself: '*What do I do to reassure myself or set things right or reduce my anxiety?*' The ritual can be an *action* (e.g. clean the object) or something you *think* (e.g. say a prayer or count to a lucky number or ponder the issue for a long time, trying to reassure yourself).

If you have been avoiding situations that trigger obsessions, answer the above questions for how you would expect to think and act in those situations. (For examples of how to apply the IBA model to analyse situations see the case studies at the end of Chapter 3).

Step 2. Identify the OCD story supporting the doubt

Select *one* of the situations you have put on your list to start working on. It is best to start with an easier situation, that is, one in which you may not believe the doubt quite as strongly, and where it is easier to resist doing the ritual. This is because working on the obsessions is a *skill*, and as with any skill, you will get better with practice – so best not to take on the toughest opponent first!

Now, take a sheet of paper and write: at the top, a brief description of the situation you selected; then below that, describe the doubt you experienced in the situation; and below that, write the heading 'OCD story'. (Alternatively, you could use the 'Obsessional doubt worksheet' provided in Appendix 3 with instructions for completing it, whichever method you prefer.)

To identify the argument supporting the doubt, or OCD story, imagine yourself being back in the situation in which you

Sonya

Sonya, whom you met in Chapter 3, drew up a list of key situations in which she experienced obsessional doubts, of which a selection is included below:

Situation 1: Cleaning the kitchen floor in the morning

Doubt: There could be dangerous germs on the floor.

Consequences: My daughter could play on the floor and get dangerously ill. It will be my fault.

Ritual: Clean thoroughly with antibacterial agent (twice over).

Situation 2: Cleaning the fridge in the morning

Doubt: There could be dangerous germs that might infect the food.

Consequences: The food will be contaminated and my daughter will get ill. It will be my fault.

Ritual: Clean thoroughly with antibacterial agent (twice over).

Situation 3: Using my telephone after lunch

Doubt: My phone could be contaminated with dangerous germs.

Consequences: I'll get the germs on my hands and infect my child. I'll be to blame.

Ritual: Ask colleague for reassurance, check and clean phone with antibacterial wipe.

Situation 4: Using the staff toilet

Doubt: It might be dirty and have germs on it.

Consequences: I'll be contaminated all over and infect my child. I'll blame only myself.

Ritual: Wipe toilet with antibacterial wipe and wash hands for five minutes afterwards in very hot water.

experienced the obsession. Picture the situation as vividly as you can to get a sense of what your thoughts were at the time when you were feeling anxious or uneasy. Ask yourself: 'Why is there a real chance that this doubt is true?' or 'Why is this doubt credible or convincing?' or 'Why is it possible that this doubt is true?'

Write down whatever enters your mind in response to this question under the heading 'OCD story', no matter how far-fetched it may seem on sober reflection. Think of anything the OCD may come up with to try and convince you that the doubt is real and likely to be true. Keep on adding further elements to the OCD story as new thoughts come into your mind, perhaps over the coming days or weeks as you may encounter the same situation again, or as you think more about the issue.

It is quite typical that the OCD story will contain a number of further doubts or *secondary doubts* (some of these may come up as you're working on the commonsense alternative to the OCD story – see below). Sometimes these will develop in a cascade as you're trying to think your way back to reassurance about the original doubt.

End off the OCD story with the statement: 'This is why I need to …' and write down the ritual that you performed in the situation to reassure yourself. After reading the OCD story, rate your level of belief or how much you believed the doubt in the situation on a 0–100% scale.

When rating your level of belief, beware of getting stuck on trying to do this 100% perfectly or accurately (and this applies to all ratings as part of the programme). The demand for perfect accuracy is simply the OCD trying to derail your programme by getting you to take obsessional doubts seriously, e.g. 'Maybe I'm not doing this in the right way' (which you fear would cause the programme to fail). Accept that your level of belief may not always be exactly the same and be content with not spending too much time deciding on your rating. The 'right' way of providing the rating is after brief consideration, and it is only meant to be a rough and ready indication of your baseline level of belief.

Step 3. Reflect on the OCD thinking devices used in the OCD story

Carefully read through the list of thinking devices listed previously in this chapter to see whether any of those might apply to your OCD story. You may also choose to read through the list of thought distortions in the table on page 21 in Chapter 2. For example, try to identify where remote imaginary possibilities lead you astray from what your senses and common sense tell you about the reality of the situation. See where facts are wheeled in and made to seem relevant to the specific situation without any direct supporting evidence. Be on the lookout for when an arbitrary or exaggerated standard for objects, activities or thoughts is being made to seem important at the expense of their function.

Consider that it may be possible to label individual statements in the OCD story with *more than one* thinking device; they are not mutually exclusive. Also, it is more important to understand the general principles underlying the OCD story (that it is removed from the immediate situation and goes against the senses and common sense) than be able to label each thinking device with 100% precision.

Sonya

Situation
Needing to use the office phone after lunch.

Obsessional doubt

'Someone could have used the phone and contaminated it with dangerous germs.'
Sonya asked herself why there was a real chance that the doubt was true, and identified the OCD story. (She also identified the OCD thinking devices and other thought distortions and put these in brackets.)

Continued

OCD story

Germs exist (wheeling in facts). You can't see them (wheeling in facts). Somebody with a cold or some other dangerous infection may have used my phone while I was out (introducing secondary doubts – I did not observe that this happened in this situation and there is no other direct evidence). Or even if they weren't ill, they could have had germs on their hands because people often don't wash their hands as frequently as they should, such as when they've used the toilet (introducing secondary doubts – I did not see any of this happen in this situation now or even in recent months). There could also be a dangerous illness going through the office with the germs being spread around, without any of the people affected knowing it yet (imaginary story).

The germs could have been transferred from their hands onto the phone (introducing secondary doubts – I did not see anybody touch the phone). Germs are dangerous (wheeling in facts; also overgeneralization – not all germs are dangerous). They can enter the body through the skin (wheeling in facts). They stay alive for a long time (overgeneralization – not all germs stay alive for a long time). The only way to kill them is by using antibacterial wipes, and even then, you may miss a patch on the phone. This is why I need to clean the phone thoroughly with an antibacterial wipe.

Level of belief in the doubt: 75%.

Step 4. Develop the commonsense view

Take a sheet of paper and write the heading 'Alternative to the doubt'. Below this write down the opposite of the obsessional doubt in one or two short sentences, suggesting that the particular object/situation/person is *OK*, and that the doubt is untrue.

Now, below the alternative to the doubt, write down the heading 'Commonsense view'. This is the argument supporting the *alternative to the doubt* you have just described. It includes all the reasons why things are in fact OK, why there is no need to worry, and why you don't need to perform your ritual.

Read through the points in the OCD story, and ask yourself what your common sense and reality tell you about each of those points. Consider what you would have told a friend describing a similar story, or what a person you trust would have thought about the matter. Try to think back to how your perspective would have been different before your OCD started. Try and remember what happened previously in your life when you didn't perform the ritual or avoid the situation, and what that tells you about the doubt. Reflect on how you think differently in situations in other areas of your life.

Write down all the commonsense points you can think of, firmly grounded in common sense and the direct evidence provided by your senses. Try to answer each point made in the OCD story. As you are writing down your commonsense points, you may find that your mind responds with a 'Yes ... but what if ...?' or 'Yes, but maybe ...' This is to be expected and each one of these 'yes ... buts' needs to be included under the OCD story, and, in turn, should be responded to in the commonsense view. (Some people prefer to develop the commonsense view point by point in response to points made in the OCD story. This is fine, but it is still preferable eventually to combine all the points made separately under the respective headings of 'OCD story' and 'Commonsense view'.)

Consider the following when working on the commonsense view:

- You need to appreciate that retraining your mind to think in a different way does not happen overnight. In the same way that the defence attorney referred to previously has to invest significant time and thought in building a strong argument to persuade the jury, you have to work patiently and creatively on your commonsense argument, thinking carefully about the points you include and adding new elements as your new perspective unfolds. Particularly where your OCD has been longstanding, you may have lost track of what the commonsense perspective is. It may then be helpful to do a small survey of the opinions of others whose opinion you value, or get information from other reputable sources. Consider carefully how these views differ from yours.

- You should expect that initially the commonsense view would not produce a 'gut feeling' sense of being true. This is because an old thinking habit can sometimes be like an old and draughty house – cold in winter and desperately in need of repairs, but still strangely comfortable and secure because it is so familiar. It takes a while for a new way of thinking to take root and start feeling familiar.

- *It is also important to consider that developing the common-sense view does not require proving the OCD story 'wrong'.* By its nature the OCD thinking devices make it very difficult or even impossible to prove the OCD story wrong by way of testing it in the normal way. For example, if you find that an obsessional doubt proves not to be true in a given situation, your OCD story will probably tell you that this does not *prove* that it may not be true in future! Also, if you manage to satisfy yourself with 100% certainty (which is usually not possible) that a remote scary possibility is not true, *there are always other remote scary possibilities at hand to start worrying about.* When the imagination is given free rein, unconstrained by immediate reality, the number of remote possibilities is unlimited and any of these could potentially be hoovered up into the OCD story! This is how the OCD story and the obsessional doubt defy attempts to disprove it.

- Your OCD may encourage you to act as if the situation (*which can't be proven safe*) is dangerous/not OK; rather than considering the situation safe (judged by the senses and common sense), until proven dangerous. One could illustrate this approach by applying it to the common situation of driving. Let's say you assumed that all other drivers on the road are actually drunk, but acting sober. You think that you cannot immediately tell if they're drunk from their driving, because they're trying their utmost to appear sober and drive in a straight line (so there is no way to 'prove' their sobriety by using the senses). But, because they're drunk, they could drive erratically at any moment and cause an accident (which means the situation is dangerous). And that's why you can't allow any car to come within 40 metres of yours at any time. Would it be possible to drive at all? I think you can see some of the pitfalls of applying this style of thinking to driving!

- The point is to become aware of how the OCD story leads you astray and to develop a different way of thinking about the situation where you are content with doing only what immediate reality and common sense require of you (which is the approach you already use in most areas of your life!).

Finally, end off the commonsense view with a statement saying 'This is why I *don't* need to …' and describe the ritual that the OCD story would require you to do to reassure yourself. It may be helpful to add a further sentence confirming that what has already been done is all that common sense requires, and try to be specific. This is because we have to accept that there may well be certain appropriate precautions, on commonsense grounds, required of people in situations where you perform too many. The point is for you to be responsible in a *productive and useful* way, rather than in the counterproductive way that the OCD is trying to sell to you.

A few examples of appropriate precautions that many people take are: When you've used the iron, unplug it and check once. When you've handled raw meat, wash your hands once, with soap, afterwards, for no longer than half a minute. When you're handling sharp objects or dangerous chemicals, lock them away from small children. When you've used the toilet, wash your hands once, with soap, for not more than a few seconds.

The following may help you to decide what an appropriate precaution is:

- Ask yourself how your commonsense perspective on the situation reasonably would require you to respond? What would be considered sufficient if you acted *only* on the direct evidence from reality?
- Consider what other trusted people do in the particular situation? If unsure about this, ask them, and record their answers. Also ask them how serious they would consider it if they failed to use the appropriate precaution, what they would expect to happen, and how they would cope with that. This would give you a sense of what people consider to be *acceptable risk* in their lives.
- Think of whether there may be guidelines from expert sources for safety in the particular situation? For example, experts do recommend that we wash our hands after handling raw meat, but not that we wash our hands three times for 10 minutes in scalding water! They also recommend that unprotected sex with a person who is HIV-positive is risky, but they do *not* say that we shouldn't touch such a person or kiss them on the cheek.
- Also consider how *important* expert sources consider such appropriate precautions to be in terms of what they're aimed at preventing. Your OCD may encourage you to think about the situation in black and white terms, i.e. 100% safe if you take the precaution, and 100% dangerous if you don't, but usually risk is somewhere on a scale of 0–100%. For example, not washing your hands after going to the toilet is not as risky as having unprotected sex with an HIV-positive person!

Caveats

- Be careful not to demand a perfect answer or solution to the questions above – in reality people may well not give exactly the same answer to your question, but usually there will be a broad consensus on important issues.
- Expect the OCD to grab the opportunity to roll further obsessional doubts in your way ('Maybe this is not the right solution …' or 'Maybe I don't know enough yet'). Be prepared to be satisfied with consulting a limited number of trusted people or resources about your questions.
- *Consult others only if there is a good commonsense reason to do so.* Remember that there is no point asking others' opinions if you already know what they are going to tell you. If you're doing this, you may be ritualizing in response to the obsessional doubt: 'Maybe I don't know anything any more' (the 'I'm completely clueless' con). This amounts to a clever ploy to get you to discount the considerable knowledge from your past experience, your present capable functioning in areas of your life unaffected by OCD, and your common sense. Also be careful about asking them to repeat their answer if you've heard those answers perfectly well. This may be in response to obsessional doubts, such as 'Maybe I didn't understand them well enough' or 'Maybe I didn't hear them right.' Or you may be trying to feel less worried about what might happen if the doubt were true, by transferring the responsibility to them (e.g. 'if something bad happened, it wouldn't be my fault because they said I should do it').
- Deal with any further obsessional doubts that may come up by including them in the OCD story and responding to them in the commonsense view.
- *Be careful that working on the commonsense view does not become a ritual.* Because the number of remote theoretical

possibilities for why the doubt may be true, is limitless, you could carry on endlessly answering these theoretical possibilities (contained in the OCD story) in your commonsense view as a way of ritualistically reassuring yourself. For example, you may find yourself endlessly delving into the past thinking about remote possibilities (the OCD story) of reasons for why you might have made a serious mistake (the doubt), and find yourself having to answer every single one of these possibilities in your commonsense view. You may find yourself covering the same ground over and over again and the same issues keep coming up (e.g. you may deal with one remote possibility after another, without 'hard evidence' from situations in the past for taking any of them seriously).

When working on the commonsense view becomes a ritual, you may be falling victim to a doubt such as 'maybe I missed something' or 'maybe I haven't done enough'. When you find yourself working unproductively on the commonsense view (perhaps when you've been working on it for weeks without a sense of making progress), try to be content with the simple and uncomplicated perspective on the issue or situation that common sense, immediate reality and 'hard evidence' offer you; then move on to the work in Chapters 6 and 7.

Sometimes your obsessional doubt may relate to the possibility of having done something horrific in the near or distant past, such as whether you attacked a person. In such cases, when developing the commonsense view, it may be helpful to consider in some depth what your senses would have told you at the time of the experience – if you actually experienced it.

Even though this may be a blood-curdling experience, you could write this down on a sheet of paper, e.g. *feeling* the knife pushing into the victim's body, *seeing* the blood spurting, *hearing* the screams, *smelling* the fear, *hearing* the body drop, and so on. You could then consider whether there was any convincing reason for discounting your common sense telling you that you have never witnessed such an event. Beware of secondary obsessional doubts in the OCD story trying to muddy the water, for example, 'Yes ... but maybe I did it, but can't remember it' (in the absence of any realistic reason for believing this – see the list of OCD thinking devices).

Sonya

Alternative to the doubt
'My phone is OK.'
After much deliberation and carefully considering each of the points in the OCD story, Sonya formulated the common-sense view (a few 'yes ... buts' came up while she was working on the commonsense view; she included these in the OCD story and responded to them below).

Commonsense view

It is true that germs exist and that you can't see them. But, the phone is in the same position I left it. It looks clean. Nobody told me that they used my phone and I didn't see anybody use my phone. I have no direct evidence from my eyes or ears that anybody did. And even if they did, that does not mean that the person who used the phone contaminated the phone with dangerous germs. I certainly didn't see anybody who definitely had a cold or flu or other infectious illness using my phone. In fact nobody in the office is so sick that they shouldn't be at work.

From what I've seen, the people who work with me wash their hands after using the toilet most if not all of the time. And even if they didn't, that wouldn't mean that any germs on their hands are necessarily dangerous – if that were the case, people would be sick all the time.

Continued

> Not all germs are dangerous. Whether a germ is dangerous also depends on your level of exposure to it and the strength of your immunity. If there were an outbreak of a dangerous illness in the office, there would be evidence in reality of this, but everybody seems fine. There is no basis in reality for believing that a dangerous illness was sweeping through the office – this possibility comes from my imagination.
>
> I therefore have no direct evidence in reality that the phone is contaminated with dangerous germs. The direct evidence suggests that the phone is clean – indeed just that, a boring, clean phone, exactly the way I left it. This is why I don't need to clean my phone.
>
> *Level of belief in the doubt: 20%.*

Step 5. Practise the commonsense view

When you are satisfied that you have covered all the points made in the OCD story, re-rate your level of belief in the obsessional doubt (0–100%), and compare this rating to your initial rating. If your level of confidence in the doubt remains unchanged, look at the commonsense view again and see if any 'yes ... buts' remain unanswered, or if there is anything further you can add.

Try to read the commonsense view three times a day *outside OCD situations*. The reason for this is that you are likely to feel more anxious, particularly initially, in the actual situation, and therefore it would make sense to be well practised in the commonsense view *before* you face the situation.

When you have done this for a week or so, and feel that you have a good understanding of the commonsense view, find some time to sit comfortably in a quiet place, trying to relax, and vividly imagine being in the situation and thinking in the commonsense way. Before you start, focus on breathing slowly and regularly and try to relax your whole body (see Appendix 5 for relaxation exercises). Think of yourself as standing on a bridge dividing reality and OCD-land, and stopping yourself at that point where you start thinking about imaginary possibilities – which is where you cross the bridge into OCD-land. If any 'yes ... buts' come up that you have difficulty answering, go back to the drawing board – write them down under the OCD story, and consider how to answer them in the commonsense view. If you felt the visualization exercise was helpful, you may choose to do it daily for a further week.

Caveats

- *Be alert to the risk that reading or thinking the commonsense view does not become part of a ritual.* This happens when you have to read or repeat it over and over again without really understanding what it means. You can draw reassurance that the commonsense story relies on direct evidence in reality, and this is all you need, so there is no need for unnecessary repetition.
- Do not unrealistically expect your belief in the obsessional doubt to go down to zero after developing and practising the commonsense view. At this stage any reduction in the belief level would be adequate progress.

At this point, you may feel ready to stop doing the ritual in the situation you've selected to work on. However, before we move on to this crucial step, it is worth examining your thoughts about the feared consequences in the situation if your obsessional doubt were true, and how we might address these to reduce your anxiety further. This is dealt with in Chapter 6.

Key points

- You become vulnerable to getting obsessional doubts when a thinking tendency that leads you to question reality and common sense, latches on to an area of low confidence.

- Obsessional doubt leads you away from common sense and the certainty of the information that your senses tell you about reality, or have told you in the past.
- The argument that supports the obsessional doubt, or OCD story, gets you to confuse reality with imaginary possibilities. You may become preoccupied with remote, imagined possibilities instead of focusing on visible and realistic threat, as you do in other areas of your life.
- The OCD story becomes compelling because it becomes a lived-in way of thinking and relies on a clever plot.
- The obsessional doubts affect only certain areas of your life – in other areas of your life you are content to rely on what your senses and your common sense tell you.
- Your OCD story will win the day if you don't develop an alternative way of thinking rooted in reality and common sense.

Examples

Next, here are some further examples of work on the obsessional doubts of the people you have already met.

Andrew

Situation
Switching light off in my bedroom.

Obsessional doubt
'Maybe it didn't click in the right way.'

OCD story
It didn't make that crisp, definite, satisfying click, which I know it can. The click was a dull, muffled sound, rather than one single sound. This is why I need to keep on clicking it until I get it right.

Continued

Alternative to the doubt

'It clicked fine.'

Commonsense view

The click was 100% fine. It sounded fine because the light went off. I saw the light going off and that is all that is required of the click. There would only be a problem if it didn't click and the light didn't go off. What the click sounded like is 100% unimportant, but the OCD story would have me believe that it is. This is why I can stop clicking when the light is off. Once is enough.

Clare

Situation

Leaving the office after I twice checked that my computer was switched off.

Obsessional doubt

'The computer may still be on.'

OCD story

I know that I checked it twice, but maybe I missed something. I can remember seeing the computer's light going off, and the computer going quiet. But I still feel unsure about this memory. Maybe my mind is playing tricks on me and the computer wasn't really switched off. Maybe I'm remembering the computer being switched off yesterday, and not today, and this is confusing me.

The mind can play tricks on a person, such as when you think you've written something, but when you look, you've written something else. Or when you look at a shape and think it's a tree, but when it moves you suddenly realize it's a man. I know my common sense tells me this is all nonsense, and I trust my common sense, but I need more than that. This is why I need to go back and check again.

Continued

Alternative to the doubt

'The computer is off.'

Commonsense view

I *saw* the computer light going off and I *heard* it go quiet. There was nothing wrong with how my eyes and ears were working in that situation. It is a different situation compared to when you make a mistake when writing quickly and absentmindedly, or when you see something at a distance.

There is no reason to distrust my memory. When you check many times that makes it difficult to have a clear memory of any single check, but my common sense still tells me that I checked it and that it was off. There is no direct evidence in reality that there is anything wrong with my brain, and that's why I can trust what my senses tell me.

There is no reason to distrust my eyes and my ears, but my OCD story is trying to get me to distrust them and imagine things. Because my OCD thinking is a habit, it will seem insufficient to trust my senses at first, but over time that will become a habit. I don't need more than that and what common sense tells me. I trust my senses in almost all areas of life, such as when I cross the road, so why shouldn't I do the same in my OCD situations? This is why I don't need to go back and check again. Once is enough.

Ahmed

Situation

Driving in my car.

Obsessional doubt

'I may have hit someone.'

OCD story

Accidents happen. Motorists do hit cyclists and pedestrians, sometimes killing them. Any sound other than that of the engine can be a person under the car. That person

Continued

could bounce off the car and onto the side of the road, or into the vegetation on the side of the road. Or if I see something out of the corner of my eye, that could have been a person swerving to avoid me, or jumping out of the way, perhaps injuring themselves, or it could be someone bouncing off the car.

I heard a strange noise when I went round the turn and saw something dark flash in the corner of my eye. The noise definitely wasn't the engine. It could have been a person I knocked over and who is now lying on the side of the road in need of urgent help. This is why I need to go back on my route and check for bodies, check the car for blood and check the newspaper for hit-and-run accidents.

Alternative to the doubt

'I didn't hit anybody.'

Commonsense view

Yes, accidents happen and hit-and-run accidents happen. Sometimes people get hurt. Cars make many different sounds other than the engine, often the dashboard and instrument panel rattle a bit. Many other sounds are caused by objects on the road – stones, differences in the texture of the road, such as tar versus gravel, or bumps or potholes in the road. No road is perfectly even.

When you drive the scenery changes constantly. There are also other people using the road and others can be seen by the side of the road, going about their business. So you will constantly see people and objects out of the corner of your eye – that's how the eye works.

There is no evidence other than the sound of the noise and the vague shape in the corner of my eye, and these could have been anything. I certainly did not have convincing evidence from my eyes and ears that I hit a person. If I did, I'd know it for certain. I didn't clearly see a person. I didn't hear a scream. I didn't hear the sound of a bicycle being banged. I didn't hear a bystander cry out. The noise would be very loud if I hit a person and I would see

Continued

clear evidence of the person being there. There would be no doubt in my mind.

I have never heard of anybody not being aware that they hit someone, or even using it as a defence in a court case. The strange noise and what I saw in the corner of my eye were just common everyday events for a motorist. There was no convincing direct evidence from my eyes and ears that I hit somebody.

My doubt causes me to use risky ways of reassuring myself, such as constantly checking my mirror to see that the cyclist is still there after I've passed him. This is unnecessary and unsafe – best to stick with the hard evidence from my eyes and ears and let the doubt be just that, an unsubstantiated OCD doubt. This is why I don't need to go back over my route, check the car for blood, or check the newspaper for hit-and-run incidents. All I need to do is to stop when there is convincing, direct evidence that I hit somebody, and this definitely didn't happen.

Mark

Situation

Cleaning my garden shears in the greenhouse. My wife walks in holding the baby.

Obsessional doubt

'I may attack the baby.' 'Maybe I'm dangerous.'

OCD story

Why do I have these violent thoughts? It must mean that I want to do what I think about doing. I know that evil people exist who do bad things. I may be one of them. One side of me knows that I'm not a violent person, but I could still be changing into a violent person without being aware of it, leading me to suddenly strike out.

My unconscious could be against me – slowly becoming stronger inside my head and changing me into a horrible person. The only thing standing in its way is my moral beliefs, and that's why I always have to be on guard. You

Continued

hear about judges and teachers being found out to be paedophiles or murderers, changing against their will.

This is why Carole and the baby need to go inside and why I need to put the shears away.

Alternative to the doubt

'There is zero chance that I will attack the baby.' 'I am not dangerous.'

Commonsense view

I'm just having a violent thought. There is no direct evidence in reality that I want to act on the thought, or that I am a violent person.

There is no evidence in reality that I am changing as a person – I'm only having thoughts with violent content. When I compare myself with a bad, horrible person who does evil things, I also have thoughts with violent content, but I don't have an attraction to violent acts, I don't fantasize about them, I don't plan to commit violent acts so I don't have an *intention* to commit violent acts, which is crucial for action. I also don't like having this thought and I care about the victim.

Judges and teachers who are convicted of paedophilia or murder wanted to do what they did at the time of the act, so there was an intention. What they didn't want is to get caught. I don't want to harm people, so I don't have an intention, which is very different to them.

There is no evidence in reality that people with healthy brains can change in this way, against their will. There is no evidence that there is anything wrong with my brain that would allow this to happen. My moral beliefs are who I am. All the direct evidence in reality points to me being a kind, considerate person and a caring father – this is what I know is important to me and what other people tell me and have told me in the past. I doubt myself because of my OCD story, and that's all there is to it. This is why I don't need Carole to take the baby inside, and why I don't need to put the shears away. Just making sure that the baby doesn't play with sharp objects is good enough.

Jenny

Situation

Walking in the street and noticing a young teenage girl's body.

Obsessional doubt

'I may have wanted to look at her body.' 'I may be sexually attracted to her.' 'I may be a paedophile.'

OCD story

Why was my attention drawn to her buttocks? It must be because I am sexually attracted to her. There are people who are attracted to children in this way and I may be one of them. I know that I am not sexually attracted to children, but maybe this is one of the first signs. With childbirth there are changes in one's hormones that can cause people to change in unpredictable ways. One example is postnatal depression, where a mother may feel that she doesn't want her baby. Maybe my hormones haven't settled properly. I heard of a mother who started hearing voices after childbirth – this shows the power of hormones. There could have been a further impact of the drugs they gave me as part of my caesarean. Those drugs are very powerful and can also influence the hormones in unexpected ways.

If I were sexually attracted to the girl, my body would show this sexual arousal – this is why I need to check my body for signs of sexual arousal. When I did this, I felt a sensation in my groin area. It didn't feel like sexual arousal, but maybe it could be the first sign of it. This means that I could have been sexually attracted to the girl. (I get anxious and upset.) I've heard that some child-molesters get upset about their problem, and this could be me.

Also, as a young child, aged about four or five years, a female friend and I touched each other's genitals on a few occasions. This could have led to abnormal sexual development and caused this problem.

Continued

Alternative to the doubt

'I am not sexually attracted to the girl.' 'I am not a paedophile.'

Commonsense view

I know that I am not sexually aroused – I am anxious, which
is very different. It is normal for people to be curious of
people's bodies and to notice them. It is also completely
acceptable and normal and natural to appreciate physical beauty, in people of both sexes.

I feel a sensation because my attention is focused on what is
happening in my body. When one focuses on the body
you'll notice all kinds of sensations. My sensation is not
pleasant at all, but is the same as when my bladder needs
emptying. I have had this sensation in many different
situations, and it is the same when I'm looking at a building or thinking about any arbitrary topic.

It is burnt into my memory that I am very fearful of looking
at certain parts of children's bodies that I think of as
being inappropriate, but this has an unintended consequence – I then can't help but notice them – this is a pre-
requisite for being able to tell myself *not* to notice them.
This is why I keep noticing those parts and remembering
that I noticed them. Therefore my attention was drawn
to that girl's buttocks, precisely because I did not want it
to, and also because she was wearing a tight skirt and
that part is quite visible. Besides, what is wrong with
appreciating the beauty of youth?

Paedophiles seek out situations where they can get close
to children for their own interest. I tend to avoid such
situations. They find thoughts and images of children
sexually exciting. I find them upsetting. They may act on
their fantasies, by exchanging sexual photos of children
with other paedophiles. I am sure that I could not allow
myself to do this, and have no need or desire to look at
sexual images of children.

Paedophilia doesn't start suddenly, and I have yet to hear of
a case that started because of pregnancy or because of

Continued

drugs given during a caesarean. My senses have told me now and in the past that I am not sexually attracted to children and that I have not sought out sexual contact with them. Paedophiles' senses tell them that they are sexually attracted to children and this desire is conscious and gripping. Curiosity in the body as a young child also doesn't mean anything; it's usually a normal part of growing up.

Finally – the direct evidence in reality tells me that I am the complete opposite of a paedophile. This is why I don't need to check my body for sexual arousal.

6

Tackling your thinking about what would happen if the doubt were true and you didn't do the ritual

The previous chapter showed us that the obsessional doubt is always *false and out of place* because it lacks a foundation in the immediate reality of the situation and common sense, and relies on an argument rooted in the imagination. You may be confused about why this chapter deals with your thinking about the consequences if the doubt were *true*, and if you did not do your ritual to make sure things are OK. What's the point of thinking about the consequences if we know the obsessional doubt is always bogus?

This is a valid point, and one has to acknowledge that the most important part of the work is on the OCD story underlying the doubt, which is dealt with in the previous chapter. You will probably find that developing the *commonsense view* reduces your anxiety by helping you to attach less importance to the doubt. However, if thinking differently about the *consequences* serves to reduce your anxiety even further, this may actually make it even easier not to perform the ritual or not avoid the situation. In this sense it represents a 'belts and braces' approach to reduce your anxiety as much as possible. This can be illustrated by comparing the following:

1. OCD story —> take doubt seriously —> ANXIETY INCREASES —> overly negative view about what would happen if the doubt were true —> ANXIETY INCREASES EVEN MORE —> very difficult to face the situation and resist doing the ritual.

2. Commonsense view on the doubt —> attach little importance to the doubt —> ANXIETY DECREASES —> realistic view on what would happen if the doubt were true —> ANXIETY DECREASES MORE —> easy to face the situation and resist doing the ritual.

But before thinking about how to lessen your anxiety, let's think about how your current way of thinking may be worsening your anxiety. This can happen in four ways: where you *overestimate* the likelihood that bad consequences will occur; where you *underestimate* your ability to cope with them if they did; where you *consider yourself more responsible* for causing them or having failed to act to prevent them, than you in fact are (i.e. inflate your own responsibility); and where you are *unfairly hard on yourself* in terms of what it would mean about you as a person if they occurred.

The following paragraphs will outline a three-step plan for working on your thinking about the expected consequences if the doubt were true, and you did *not* do the ritual.

Step 1. Identify your current view

Take a different page to the one you used previously for working on the OCD story, and write at the top: 'Expected consequences if the doubt were true', and below that, 'Current view'. (Alternatively, you could use the 'Feared consequences worksheet' provided in Appendix 3 with instructions for completing it, whichever method you prefer.)

As suggested in Chapter 5, you have previously briefly described your thoughts about the feared consequences, but to make sure that you get all your thoughts on this topic down under 'Current view', try the following: Imagine being in the situation where you experienced the obsessional doubt as vividly as you can. Now think of all the bad consequences (or negative events) that might follow if you *didn't* perform the ritual and if the doubt were *true*. Write down the thoughts and images that enter your mind. Ask yourself the following questions:

- What will/can go wrong?
- How likely is that to happen?
- How would I cope?
- How would others affected cope?
- How much would I be to blame?
- What would that mean about me?

Rate your level of fear about the consequences on a 0–100% scale.

Sonya

Sonya, whom you met previously, continued her work on the situation at work where she experienced an obsessional doubt that her phone might be contaminated with dangerous germs. She identified her current view on the feared consequences if the doubt were true and she didn't perform the ritual as follows:

Current view (if the doubt were true)

I will be contaminated with germs – viruses or bacteria – if I touch the phone. The germs will cross through my skin into my bloodstream or get into my body when my hands touch my mouth. Even though I may wash my hands, I'll still be infectious. When touching my child at home I may infect her with a dangerous illness – you know how vulnerable children are. Who knows what will happen. If she comes to harm because of my carelessness in not taking appropriate precautions, I won't be able to forgive myself. I'll be a careless and neglectful mother.

Level of fear about the consequences: 80%.

Step 2. Develop the realistic view

Below your work under 'Current view', write the heading 'Realistic view'. Read the list of thought distortions in Chapter 2 and see if any of these appear in your current view. Now consider the following questions (not all the questions may be equally applicable to every feared consequence you work on).

What do reality and common sense tell me about the likelihood that these consequences will occur?

When answering this question consider the following:

- When calculating probabilities, the correct method is to multiply the probabilities of all the events required in the chain. For example, if Clare wanted to calculate the chance that her office building will burn down after she left her computer switched on, she needs to do it in the following way: if there is a 1/1000 chance that the electrical system is faulty, a 1/100 chance that the sprinkler system doesn't work and a 1/100 chance that the night watchman is not on his post, the chance of a major fire is $1/1000 \times 1/100 \times 1/100$, which is 1/10,000,000; that is, one in ten million! If you used this method to calculate the odds, how does that compare with the estimate provided under 'Current view'? (adapted from Van Oppen and Arntz, 1994).
- If you think that there is a high probability of the feared event occurring, ask yourself what an average, sensible person would think about this? Would this person disagree with your estimate? If so, ask yourself what you could gain from their perspective.
- Also, think about the following: what would one expect the world to look like if there was indeed a high likelihood of the feared event occurring? For example, what would you expect the world to look like if there was a good chance that

red spots on objects in public spaces were actually blood, which could infect people with dangerous illnesses? Maybe this level of risk would require cleaners to wear protective suits covering all of their bodies while on the job? And maybe those same cleaners would have little chance of successfully applying for life insurance because of the high level of risk associated with their jobs?

- If the level of precaution that people take in the real world, does not match up to the level of danger that you consider to be posed by the situation, ask yourself what this could mean. Do such people (such as the cleaners referred to in the example above) not care about their health and safety in a reckless and irresponsible way, or is it possible that the situation is less risky than you think it may be?

- Are you ignoring barriers preventing the feared event developing? For example, are you ignoring the protective role of your own immune system, or the immune system of a loved one, in protecting against infection? Do you think of your immune system as a bow and arrow while in fact it may be more like a battery of cannons? (The immune system is in fact an extraordinarily capable system). Or, are you ignoring mechanical safeguards, such as a safety switch to turn off the kettle, or other built-in safeguards in electrical appliances?

- Be careful to examine whether you may hold a *negative prejudice* about yourself suggesting that bad things are particularly likely to happen to YOU, such as that you have bad luck or always mess up or do the wrong thing. Use the guidelines on pages 65–9 in Chapter 4 to carefully examine such beliefs and formulate alternatives that provide a better reflection of reality and help you not to fall victim to a false stereotype of yourself.

- Consider whether there may be an unacknowledged benefit associated with what you fear may happen; for example, it is now known that some exposure to germs may in fact benefit the development of children's immune systems, and some bacteria are helpful for the digestive process in humans.

Am I underestimating my or others' ability to cope with the consequences?

- What do objective reality and common sense tell you about your ability to deal effectively with a feared situation, if it did arise? Are there safeguards already in place that would prevent a catastrophe; for example, house insurance if your house flooded or burnt down, car insurance if your car got stolen, or appropriate medical treatment if you developed a serious medical condition?
- What does your coping in past difficult situations allow you to predict reasonably about your ability to cope in future difficult situations? For example, it may be reasonable to expect that if you coped with your car being stolen in the past, or your child being sick, you will be able to do so again in the future. This may well be an unpleasant experience or an inconvenience, but does not have to be catastrophic.
- Again be careful not to be prejudiced against yourself in a negative way; for example, believing yourself to be incompetent and helpless, whereas when you think objectively about how you coped with difficult situations in the past, or when you ask others to rate your ability, a more favourable picture presents itself. Similarly, be careful when telling yourself that the feared event will be the *worst possible thing in the world* (catastrophizing) and that, if it happened, you *absolutely couldn't stand it* (low frustration tolerance). On reflection the event may only be very unpleasant or inconvenient – not devastating – and there may be little reason to believe that you couldn't tolerate it.
- Also, try not to catastrophize on others' behalf or to underestimate them, believing that an event would be disastrous

in their lives when there is little objective reason for taking such a dim view. Even if *they* were to catastrophize, it doesn't mean *you* have to agree with them!

Am I taking more responsibility for the bad consequences than I need to?

Responsibility reflects your sense of which actions are reasonably required of you to prevent something bad from happening to yourself or others. The implication is that you could be criticized or blamed if something went wrong because you did not live up to your responsibilities; that is, you did not do what you should have done to prevent the event from happening. A researcher in London, Professor Paul Salkovskis, has shown that people with OCD frequently consider themselves as bearing a heavier burden of responsibility for preventing bad consequences in situations they perceive to be risky, than those without OCD. This may well contribute to an increased sense of danger and higher levels of anxiety in those situations.

Therefore it would be a good idea to consider how accountable you would be, or how much you would be to blame, if the feared consequences occurred. This is, of course, assuming that the doubt was true (which invariably it isn't) and the consequences occurred because you didn't perform the ritual.

Generally people tend to be blamed *more* when the following circumstances apply and tend to be blamed less (or not at all) if the reverse applies:

- You were specifically assigned the responsibility (although, even if you were specifically assigned the responsibility, it would be unfair to hold you accountable for very unexpected consequences arising from your action – that is, if the next point below didn't apply).
- There is a realistic possibility of the feared consequences arising in the situation, if you left the situation unattended;

and, if this is the case, one can realistically expect that the feared consequences are likely to be very bad.
- There are clear and immediate signs of danger or risk in the situation.
- You are the sole person whose actions (or lack of action) contributed to the feared consequences arising.

For example, consider the following: imagine walking down the high street of a bustling town. You notice a plastic bag on the pavement. You think: 'What if I leave it there and a small child picks up the plastic bag and puts it in her mouth or over her head and chokes or smothers, and dies. I'd be a murderer!'

Your thinking in the situation would place all the blame squarely on yourself. However, a more fair and objective perspective on your responsibility would be as follows: you weren't designated the responsibility of picking up plastic bags in that situation. Although it is in theory possible that a child may in fact choke on or smother herself with the plastic bag, it is extremely unlikely (parents or minders look after very small children and the older ones would be able to avoid choking or smothering). You haven't seen any children putting the plastic bag in their mouths or over their heads (no clear and immediate sign of danger). Even in case of this eventuality, certainly many others would be held accountable (e.g. the parents or childminder, the town council for inadequate cleaning, etc.). Your average reasonable person would not blame you for the child's death.

However, the situation would be very different if you were working as a childminder for very young children (designated responsibility), you notice a child playing and putting a plastic bag over her head (there is a reasonable likelihood of the child smothering and there is a clear sign of danger), and you are the only person looking after that child (you are the sole person responsible). If the child smothered and died you'd face a very large part of the blame.

Therefore I suggest carefully considering each of the above issues in as far as they inform how much you would be to blame in a situation if the obsessional doubt were true and the feared consequences occurred (e.g. the computer caught fire after you left it switched on, or a child was fatally injured by a piece of glass that you left on the pavement).

The following may be helpful:

- Approach a sensible person whose opinion you value and describe in some detail the situation where the feared consequences occurred. Ask them if they were the person in the situation to what extent they would consider themselves responsible and how much they would be to blame? What would they say to a friend finding him or herself in that unfortunate situation?
- How would a judge in a court of law apportion the responsibility?
- Would there be mitigating factors, or factors that reduce the level of accountability? Would others share the responsibility?
- A method for examining your thinking about who should share in the responsibility for an incident is described next.

List all the people and institutions whose actions may contribute to a negative event occurring and assign a percentage reflecting the size of their contribution, adding up to 100%. Then draw a pie chart to illustrate how the responsibility is divided between them (this is done by drawing a circle and dividing the circle into segments of different sizes according to the percentage of responsibility of each person or institution). Think in both specific (e.g. specific people and agencies) and global terms about who should be sharing the blame (e.g. the department of health for not warning more comprehensively about the risk of contaminated foods, or electronics companies for not doing more rigorous checks for faulty wiring, etc.). To illustrate this for the situation referred to above, Clare drew the pie chart on page 141 in this chapter (figure 5).

Caveats

Be careful not to confuse responsibility for doing something (or for failing to do it) with responsibility for the consequences of doing something (or of failing to do it). These are not the same and are easily confused. (For example: 'I did it and nobody else; so I must be responsible for everything that followed.') Responsibility for an action depends on our decision to perform the action – if we do (or don't), then we are responsible for performing the action (or not performing it). However, it is a separate issue to which extent we are to blame for what happens as a consequence of the action or not performing the action (i.e. how responsible or accountable we are held for the consequences).

For example, you may be responsible for accidentally dropping a sheet of paper as you are walking along, but no reasonable person would consider you to blame for the fact that it might have blown on to a motorway, causing an accident. This would be considered a freak accident; that is, a sequence of connected events which nobody could reasonably have anticipated, and therefore nobody is to blame.

As you can see it is an altogether more complicated issue to determine your level of responsibility for the consequences of your action, as opposed to your responsibility for the action. In the case of responsibility for performing the action, it is best thought of as falling into one of two categories: either you're responsible or you're not, and in the case of responsibility for the consequences, it is best considered as falling somewhere on a line between 0% and 100%, depending on the contribution of the four issues listed above.

Be careful not to think in black and white terms about your responsibility for preventing harm. Any situation in life presents you with a thousand opportunities for taking action to prevent remote possibilities of harm to self or others. It is almost never possible to do all that you can do to eliminate remote possibilities of harm. That is why society draws a compromise by recommending taking precautions when there is *real danger or risk*. It would be an unreasonable and unattainable expectation of members of society to act to prevent *all* remote possibilities of harm in *all* situations, and therefore society does not expect that of you!

Be careful of the 'lone ranger complex'; that is, thinking of yourself as the only person capable of the foresight required to protect others from harm. Try not to underestimate their abilities and allow them the right and privilege of thinking and fending for themselves!

Am I being unfairly hard on myself in terms of what it would mean about me as a person if the worst happened?

For the sake of argument, let's assume the worst: the doubt is true and bad consequences follow. What would that mean about you as a person? Is it possible that you may be overly hard on yourself? Is it possible that you may see this as simply confirming a negative prejudice you already hold about yourself (also discussed in the first two questions above), itself relying on negatively distorted views of reality? (You may choose to reread the guidelines on pages 65–9 in Chapter 4 on how to work on negative underlying beliefs). The point of examining this question is not to change your values: it may be very important to you to be a kind person who takes care not to harm others or someone who is precise and does a thorough job; you may take your responsibilities seriously, and nobody would want you to change that! However, it may be worth reconsidering your views if it turns out that you did any of the following:

- Apply double standards. Ask yourself how you would judge another person in a similar situation? If your 'judgement' on such a person is kinder than your judgement of yourself, you may well be applying double standards – judging others kindly, and making allowances for their unavoidable human fallibility, but perhaps being unfairly harsh and critical towards yourself!
- Reaching blanket negative conclusions about yourself as a *person* on the basis of *one instance* of not living up to your expectations (see the list of thought distortions in Chapter 2). Carefully considering the complexity of yourself and your life would allow a kinder judgement. One instance of 'failure' or 'bad behaviour' does not make YOU a failure or a bad person.

Sonya

Sonya previously formulated her current view on the consequences (see above). See how she formulated the realistic view below.

Realistic view

My immune system protects me 24/7 against microscopic organisms. My skin is also a barrier against germs. My immune system and skin protect me against a multitude of contacts with germs over the course of the day. My three-year-old also has an immune system and skin protecting her. Some exposure to germs is thought to be helpful for the development of children's immune systems. So even if I did unintentionally expose her to germs, that wouldn't necessarily be bad for her.

Whether an infection develops, depends on how many viruses or bacteria the person is exposed to, and whether their immune function is low or not; for example, people who are HIV-positive may be very vulnerable to infections, because their immune function is low. Neither my

Continued

daughter nor I have conditions that would cause our immune systems to malfunction.

Even if anybody became ill, which may happen from germs carried by food, touch or air, the doctors are very good at treating infectious conditions. Our society is also very good about preventing infections and epidemics, and if office phones were dangerous, they'd have warnings all over them, like cigarette boxes. I don't see any warnings on office phones.

My daughter has had colds and infections before and managed to get through them. They were definitely unpleasant, but not disastrous. She coped, and all kids get the odd cold or infection.

Nobody expects me to decontaminate the phone every time I use it. In fact nobody else does it, and most of them are people with loved ones and children they care about deeply. I certainly wouldn't consider any of them irresponsible or reckless. My boss expects me to get on with it, not spend hours cleaning office equipment, and that's not unreasonable. Nobody would think it my responsibility to clean the phone every time before using it.

Nobody would blame me if my child developed an infection. They'd only blame me if I did something really silly, like not feeding her proper food or not taking her to the doctor if there was something really wrong, like a bad fever, or if the house was dirty in a way that worried other people. Everybody who knows me thinks of me as a loving mum who tries my best. I also don't need to be perfect, because nobody is.

Level of fear about the consequences: 45%.

Step 3. Practise the realistic view

Read the thoughts listed under 'Realistic view' and rerate your level of fear about the consequences on a 0–100% scale. You may find that thinking more realistically translates into a reduction in your rating. Alternatively, you may find that there is no reduction in your rating. For example, Mark has an obsessional doubt about attacking his baby. When reflecting on his thinking about the consequences if he did in fact harm the baby, he acknowledged that he might have been overestimating some of the negative consequences (see the end of this chapter). But the prospect of harming the baby was still so upsetting to him that he gained little relief from this change in perspective. Harming his baby still obtained a 100% rating. This suggests that in Mark's case, the most important work on his OCD needs to be focused on the OCD story underlying the doubt (which is covered in the previous chapter).

However, if there is a reduction in your rating, practise the realistic view on the consequences *in addition* to the common-sense view on the doubt, by first reading it a number of times a day until you have a thorough understanding of it and then visualizing yourself thinking in that way in the situation (steps described in Chapter 5). You may find that when you are ready to face the situation, this exercise will have helped to reduce the anxiety you experience in the situation, making it easier not to do the ritual. Below the key points of this chapter you will find some examples of work done by the people you have already met on their thinking about what they expect to happen if the doubt were true.

Key points

- Overly negative thinking about the consequences if your doubt were true, and you didn't perform the ritual, may worsen your anxiety.
- You may overestimate the likelihood that bad consequences will occur.
- You may underestimate your or others' ability to cope with the consequences if they did occur.
- You may think of yourself as more responsible for the consequences than you actually are.

- You may be unfairly hard on yourself in terms of what it would mean about you as a person if the worst actually happened.

Examples

Below are further examples of the work on the feared consequences done by the people you have already met, which continue the work on the situations they started working on in Chapter 5.

Andrew

Current view (if my doubt were true)

I will lose control over my environment. If I stop trying before getting the switch to click right, I will be so upset that I won't be able to sleep. Not sleeping is dangerous. I've heard of a condition where people can't sleep, which can result in death. Sleeplessness is also a symptom of some mental illnesses. If I get upset to the point of being unable to sleep, I could lose all control and end up in a mental asylum. That would make me a nutcase for life.

Realistic view

Controlling how the light clicks is completely, utterly unimportant and does not mean anything significant about my environment or me. Control becomes important only when it affects how well you function in the world, and the world will tell you which forms of control are important. Important areas of control are about whether I can find things when I need them, doing assignments well and handing them in on time, not losing my possessions or wasting money, and treating other people decently.

It is true that sleeplessness is sometimes a symptom of mental illness, but it is a symptom rather than a cause. Many people without mental illnesses also have insomnia and just put up with it. I have had insomnia in the

Continued

past and felt a bit rough the next day, but put up with it and didn't become unhinged.

There is no evidence that I suffer from a condition where I'm completely unable to sleep. Nobody has diagnosed me with such a condition. All the evidence tells me that insomnia is unpleasant, not dangerous. If I lose sleep, I will catch up at a later stage. To improve my sleep, I can do sensible things, such as cut down on coffee, do exercise and do relaxation exercises.

Even if the worst possible thing comes true – being admitted to a psychiatric hospital – this would not necessarily mean that I would be a 'nutcase for life'. Many mental illnesses can be treated, and many successful people have had episodes of mental illness and even spells in psychiatric hospitals.

Clare

Current view (if my doubt were true)

If my computer has been left on, it may heat up. I have seen how warm it gets after you've left it on for a while. If left on over the course of the night, there may be an electrical failure, like a short-circuit, and a fire could start. If it catches fire, it is possible that the sprinkler system is not activated – those systems do malfunction, don't they?

At the same time the night watchman may have gone to the toilet, or be doing who knows what, and the fire may spread uncontrollably. The building will burn down, all those important legal files and documents will be lost and someone may get hurt – all my fault! I'd be sacked and end up jobless, a complete failure and a waste of space.

Realistic view

It is true that the power box heats up after a while. But it is designed not to cause electrical faults that may cause a

Continued

fire. In fact, lots of careful time and planning go into designing electrical equipment, and the products have to meet lots of specifications to ensure safety. I have never heard of a fire started by a computer left on overnight.

Nobody in my office seems to worry too much about leaving their computers on – most of them switch theirs off in the evening, but I haven't seen anybody too worried if they don't or come back to check if they've done so. On odd occasions someone has left their computer on, but nobody made too much of a fuss about it. The only fuss is about saving electricity. If it were dangerous to leave your computer on, there would have been huge signs reminding you to do that. People would have been very nervous about leaving them on. Possibly computers wouldn't even have been allowed for use in office buildings, if they were dangerous for starting fires. I don't see any signs like that, so they must be safe.

Even if I think of all the possibilities that have to occur for a major fire to start, and I try to calculate the odds for this chain of events, it would look like this: if there is a 1/1000 chance that the wiring is faulty, a 1/100 chance that the sprinkler system doesn't work and a 1/100 chance that the night watchman is not on his post, the chance of a major fire is 1/1000 x 1/100 x 1/100, which is 1/10,000,000 on my calculator. That is one in ten million – very unlikely!

In the tiny event of a major fire starting, it is also not true that I would be to blame for everything. The computer company would be to blame for the faulty electrical wiring, the company responsible for the servicing of office fire-prevention equipment would be to blame for the sprinkler system that didn't work, and the care-taker would be to blame for not being at his post. A pie chart for how much of the responsibility is mine, would look like:

Continued

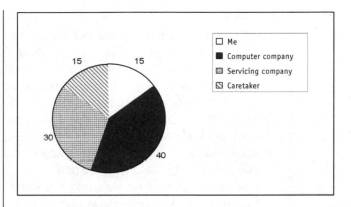

Figure 5 Clare's pie chart

Fact is, not all of it will be my fault. Everybody knows how
conscientious I am. My boss wouldn't sack me for forgetting to do something which most of the other staff also
forget on occasion. Even the partners sometimes forget
to switch off electrical equipment.

Even if the worst happens – making one mistake leading to
disastrous consequences and being sacked for it, this
would not mean that I am *100%* a failure or a waste of
space. It would mean that I made one mistake. There is
little reason to expect that I will never be able to find a
job again.

Ahmed

Current view (if my doubt were true)

If I hit a cyclist and didn't attend to her, I'd be arrested for
a hit-and-run accident and sent to prison. I won't survive
there. Everybody knows what happens in prisons –
inmates get beaten up and sexually assaulted. The
tabloids will have me for breakfast – my photo will be all
over the front page. They'd call me a monster!

Continued

Realistic view

I don't have a criminal record and no history of serious accidents, so the judge may pass a light sentence. There would also be plenty of evidence of my anxieties about harming anybody. My wife and doctor would testify to that. My wife always complains that I am driving too slowly. It may be considered that I am a Muslim and don't drink alcohol. Perhaps the judge would be persuaded to call it an unfortunate mistake. The tabloids may run a story on someone whose worst fear came true, rather than about me being a monster, because everybody who knows me knows that I'm not a monster. That would make a better story as well. Also, more importantly – I know I'm not a monster. I still don't believe I could survive prison and would rather not think about it.

Mark

Current view (if my doubt were true)

If I hurt my baby in any way, I will destroy all that is precious to me! My wife will divorce me and I will be sent to prison for life. I won't be able to live with the guilt. I'd be the worst kind of murderer.

Realistic view

It is true that hurting my child would be horrific. There's no getting away from that. And it would be horrible to live with the guilt afterwards. It is also very likely that my wife would leave me. But, I'm not sure I'd be sent to prison – maybe the judge would consider diminished responsibility on the basis of mental illness, and I won't be convicted of murder. Everybody knows how much I care about the baby. I've always acted kindly towards children.

Jenny

Current view (if my doubt were true)

If people knew that I was a paedophile, I'd be shunned and rejected by society. My family would distance themselves from me. I'll turn into something sick and repulsive.

Realistic view

People would only know if I told them about my thoughts, which I simply wouldn't do. I'd only get into trouble with the police if I acted on my thoughts, and I'm 100% sure that I wouldn't do that. My partner has been impatient sometimes when I asked him for reassurance, but he is sympathetic about my battle with the thoughts, so he wouldn't reject me. And even if the worst happened, that wouldn't undo all the kind things I've done for people in my life.

7

Facing the situation without performing the ritual

In the previous chapters we've looked at aspects of your OCD thinking that explain why you feel such a strong urge to perform the ritual. You've considered how the argument (or OCD story) supporting the obsessional doubt, and your thinking about the feared consequences if the doubt were true, combine to make you feel anxious or uneasy about things not being OK and what may happen as a consequence. The OCD 'solution' to coping with these unpleasant feelings is to do a ritual to get reassurance or to avoid the situation altogether.

You've also discovered that the OCD story leads you away from the certainty of the direct evidence from your senses in reality, and common sense, and that your thoughts about what would happen if the doubt were true may make the feared consequences seem worse than they need be. You've done work on developing a commonsense view as an alternative to the OCD story, and on developing a realistic view as opposed to your current view on the feared consequences. You are likely to have found that your level of conviction in the doubt has decreased, and that the feared consequences are not as fearsome or realistic compared with how they seemed to you previously. Your new way of thinking, firmly rooted in reality and common sense, will help to reduce your anxiety and unease about the obsessional situation, and make it easier to feel that it isn't necessary to do the ritual. (See figure 6 to remind you of how the work in Chapter 7 builds on the work in Chapters 5 and 6.)

However, old ways of thinking and acting die hard. Think how you would struggle if traffic lights were changed for red to mean 'go' and for green to mean 'stop'! We have to recognize that changing our way of thinking is not like a bolt of lightning, changing everything instantly. It is a gradual process and is similar to a seesaw slowly tilting to the other side. For this reason, despite your work on different ways of thinking, it is to be expected that you may still experience anxiety when you decide to stop the ritual.

Another reason why you may continue to experience anxiety when you encounter the situation that prompts your obsessional doubt, is a process called *fear conditioning*. This means that, through your OCD story and your thinking about the feared consequences if the doubt were true, you have eventually become conditioned to experience a feeling of anxiety or unease almost automatically whenever you encounter the situation. Despite having developed a different way of thinking, which reduces your anxiety, some of this conditioned (or imprinted) anxiety may persist stubbornly.

Be careful that this conditioned anxiety doesn't lead you to fall victim to 'emotional reasoning' (described in Chapter 2). This happens when you experience conditioned anxiety and then look around for a hook to hang it on – this involves reasoning that because you are still feeling anxious, and for no other realistic reason, there must be danger. Trust your senses and common sense to tell you whether objectively there is danger in the situation.

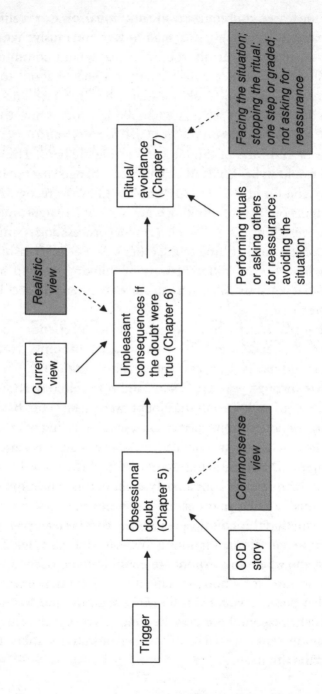

Figure 6 How cognitive track CBT fits together

The best way of getting rid of the remaining anxiety is to expose yourself repeatedly to the situation and not perform the ritual until the conditioning wears off and your anxiety eventually disappears completely. Ways of making this final step are described below.

Be careful not to be tempted because of your progress in changing your OCD *thinking*, that it therefore doesn't matter if you didn't stop doing the rituals or stopped avoiding difficult situations. This line of thinking simply represents further clever ways in which the OCD charlatan may be trying to seduce you into not letting him give up his prized possessions – your time, effort, freedom and life enjoyment. Remember OCD will not help you to achieve your life goals. Ditching the ritual and reducing avoidance are therefore crucial steps, which cannot be sidestepped or avoided and should preferably not be delayed without good reason.

Ditching the ritual

If you feel that your level of belief in the doubt (i.e. how much you believe the doubt) has decreased to a low level and you feel little anxiety about not doing the ritual, then go ahead and face the situation without doing the ritual (the one-step approach). I would recommend doing this if your belief level in the doubt is *20% or below*, and if your estimated rating of your anxiety in the situation, if you didn't do the ritual, is *50% or below*. If, however, your belief in the doubt is *40% or below* and your anxiety is *50% or above* you may choose to use a graded approach. If your belief in the doubt continues to be *above 40%*, I suggest doing more work in the way described in Chapter 5 on the OCD story feeding into the doubt, and the commonsense view, to allow your belief level to decrease further.

If after having done further work, you find that your belief in the doubt resolutely remains *above 40%*, I suggest exposing yourself to the situation without performing the ritual, using the graded approach. This can serve as a final powerful way of testing the OCD story and bolstering the commonsense view further, by allowing you to reflect carefully afterwards on the new information that you have gathered from this experience (see below).

When using either approach, *before facing the situation and not doing the ritual*, it is important to have a thorough grasp of the commonsense view on the doubt (Chapter 5) and the realistic view on what would happen if the doubt were true and you didn't perform the ritual (Chapter 6).

Caveat

Beware of demanding 100% certainty about the remote possibility represented in the obsessional doubt not being possible, before ditching the ritual or facing the situation. This demand is yet another thinking trick used by the OCD to lasso you and pull you back into OCD-land just as you were preparing to make your escape. Instead, it makes more sense to accept that we live our lives in the omnipresence of an infinite number of possibilities for things to go wrong or be awry in one way or another, and to opt for full and wholehearted engagement with the opportunities that life affords us and deal vigorously with problems if and when they arise. This attitude is represented in the decision to act according to what your senses and common sense tell you in the situation, and this being all you need.

The one-step approach: what to do in the situation

The following guidelines will help you to deal with obsessional doubts if and when you experience them in the situation:

- When an obsessional doubt comes into your mind, think of yourself as standing on a bridge separating two worlds: on the one side reality and on the other side the imagination.

- Focus your attention on the direct evidence from reality, and the certainty of what your senses and your common sense tell you about the situation and the doubt. Do this briefly, once only and without any special effort.
- Reassure yourself that this is all you need. Any attempt to get more information will involve crossing into OCD-land, with its shadowy and blurred thinking.
- Reflect on the sharp pull to cross the bridge into OCD-land making you feel as if you're not doing enough to control the situation. Realize that this is imaginary and that there is reassuring certainty in reality and common sense, and that this is all you need. There is no need to cross the bridge.
- Now, act on the information from your senses and your common sense, dismiss the obsessional doubt and do not perform the ritual. If you have previously decided on an *appropriate precaution* (see Chapter 5), do this instead.

When you're doing the above the first few times, you may have difficulty *really* trusting yourself and looking at what is there. This is to be expected and is because the OCD is trying to lure you into OCD-land and do more than you need to do. Remember that trusting your senses and your common sense is allowing them to tell you what is there, or what is important, in a natural way – exactly the same as in other situations, like crossing the road. Therefore try not to cross into OCD-land in the following ways:

- Looking too intently or for too long (staring) – this involves putting in too much effort.
- Looking too quickly – this creates uncertainty which will activate your imagination.
- Allowing the imagination to impose itself on vague information from the senses and confuse you with 'what ifs ...' by using OCD thinking devices, e.g. a vague spot in the corner

of your eye when driving becomes a body bouncing off the windscreen, or a light reflecting on a computer screen becomes a power indicator light which is switched on (both are examples of confusing the links between objects or items – see the list of OCD thinking devices in Chapter 5).

Practice the above repeatedly in the obsessional situation. The more you do this, the more your confidence will grow and the easier you will find it to tackle situations that used to be difficult. You will quickly find that the obsessions will become less frequent and less intense. Practice this new confident way of thinking and acting in the knowledge that you are simply reclaiming a time-tested and effective approach that you already use in many other areas of your life.

Using a graded approach

Using a graded approach is like getting into a swimming pool by first putting in one foot, then your other foot, then getting onto the step and slowly walking in from the shallow end until you are fully submerged. The discomfort of being exposed to the cold water may last longer than when jumping in at the deep end, but it is less of a shock because you have to cope with less discomfort at any one single moment. In a similar way you may stand to benefit from ceasing to do your ritual, or reducing your avoidance of the situation, by breaking this major step down into a series of smaller steps.

In order to do this, consider your ritual carefully and reread the commonsense view on the doubt you developed previously, to remind you what an *appropriate* precaution in the situation is – as opposed to the ritual. This appropriate level of precaution then becomes your target, and the aim of your graded approach is to gradually reduce your ritual to the level of an appropriate precaution (or perhaps none is needed). Or think of different steps, ranked from easier to more difficult, for immersing yourself fully in the situation, without safeguards. There are different ways of grading this process in terms of difficulty, and deciding on what would be the easier intermediate steps between the ritual and your final target. The following are examples:

- Rate the number of times you check an appliance (= x number of times). Reduce the number of times you check on a daily basis; for example, on the first day, check x minus 1 number of times, on the second day, check x minus 2 number of times, and so on until you check once only.
- Rate the number of times you wipe an object and then reduce this in the same way as described above.
- Measure how long you take to wash your hands. On the first day wash 20 seconds shorter, on the second day a further 20 seconds shorter, and so on, until you reach your target of 20 seconds only.
- Gradually increase how much of your body surface you expose to a public toilet, and the time interval between using the toilet and having a shower.
- Check the local daily newspaper for reports of hit-and-run accidents, for the first week every second day, and for the second week, every fourth day, and so on until you stop checking completely.
- Arrange an increasing array of items in your cupboard flexibly, in a way which emphasizes the commonsensical function of organizing things in that way, rather than according to an arbitrary rule with little relation to function.

For each of the intermediate steps where you do progressively less of the ritual, follow the guidelines outlined under 'The one-step approach' to cope with any obsessional doubts you may experience.

pedestrian while driving in daylight, Ahmed continued to experience doubts while driving at night. This made it necessary for Ahmed to work on the situation of driving at night in exactly the same way as he did for the situation of driving by day.

If you experience obsessional doubts that are quite different – for example, doubts about contamination *and* doubts about appliances being switched off – it becomes important to do a separate piece of work for each doubt. In this case you simply need to repeat the steps outlined in Chapters 5–7 for situations within which you experience either doubt. Below the key points you will find examples of how our individuals with OCD worked on their rituals.

Key points

- Despite your work on new ways of thinking in obsessional situations, you may continue to feel anxious in situations that prompt the obsessional doubt. This is because old thinking habits die hard and because fear conditioning has caused you to feel anxious automatically.
- The best way of getting rid of any remaining anxiety is to expose yourself repeatedly to the situation and not perform the ritual.
- You can stop performing the ritual in one single step, or make it easier by stopping the ritual according to a series of smaller steps.
- Before stopping the ritual, it is essential to have a good understanding of the commonsense view on the doubt and the realistic view on what would happen if the doubt were true and you did not perform the ritual.
- When facing the situation, think of yourself as standing on a bridge separating two worlds: on the one side is reality and common sense, and on the other side, the OCD shadow land

of imaginary possibilities. Try to stay in reality and dismiss the obsessional doubt.

- Do not cross into OCD-land by being caught up in staring, looking too quickly, or allowing the imagination to impose 'what ifs' on ambiguous information.
- Reflect on what you've learned about the doubt and about your anxiety in the situation, after not performing the ritual.

Examples

Prior to working on their rituals, all the people discussed below did extensive work on developing a commonsense view on their obsessional doubt, as an alternative to the OCD story. They also developed a realistic view to their current view on the expected feared consequences if the doubt were true. While in the situation, they practised coping with the obsessional doubt and not doing the ritual by using the steps described above.

Sonya

After completing the written work on her OCD thinking, Sonya's belief in the doubt was 20% and her anxiety 15%. However, she still preferred to opt for a graded approach to stopping the ritual, rather than the one-step approach, saying that she preferred this because the ritual had become such a part of her life.

She aimed to change the ritual over three-day periods. Over the first three-day period she stopped closely examining the phone when she got back from lunch. She simply gave it a brief, but attentive glance, though she still wiped it. Over the second three days she stopped asking her colleagues for reassurance. Over the third three days she stopped wiping the phone with antibacterial wipes. Thereafter all she did was give the phone a casual glance, and she eventually even stopped doing that. She acknowledged that her anxiety increased at the beginning of every phase, but found that it reduced rapidly as she got on with her day and reassured herself that her senses did not provide her with any reason to be worried about the phone.

After overcoming her obsessions about the phone, she started on her OCD story supporting her doubt about using the office toilet.

Andrew

Andrew worked carefully on his commonsense view about the click of the light switch. He also found his anxiety about not doing the ritual considerably reduced after he considered his thoughts about the consequences if the doubt were true, and developed the realistic view. At this point, Andrew decided that it was all quite unnecessary. He stopped his ritual in one attempt. Initially he had the occasional fleeting obsession about the sound of the click come into his mind, but he dismissed it easily. Over time he stopped thinking completely about what the click sounded like.

Andrew also made rapid progress with his obsessional doubts in other areas. He discovered that in those other situations the OCD stories, and his thoughts about the consequences if the doubt were true, had considerably overlapped with his OCD thoughts about the light switch. His mood improved and his general anxiety eased somewhat, allowing him to focus on his computer course and finding a job.

Clare

Clare found that her belief in the doubt of the computer being on, after having checked it once, reduced to 15% when she thought about this when being outside the situation. Her anxiety was 20%. At this point she decided to face the situation and worked late one evening, intending to be the last person in the office to leave. She opted for the one-step approach. However, when closing the door after having checked the computer once, she found her anxiety had soared (to 70%) and the obsessional doubt was quite strong (60%). She therefore decided rather to back off, check once more and leave it for a later day.

Clare then went back to her written OCD work, added a few more details to her commonsense view on the doubt and her realistic view on the consequences, and practised it daily, as suggested in Chapters 5 and 6. On reflection, she also realized that the day that she initially chose for stopping the ritual was a particularly busy and stressful day, and that this didn't help her anxiety. She therefore waited for a more relaxed day when she chose to face the situation again. She checked once, and had to stop herself from staring at the computer light by thinking about standing on the bridge, and opting for reality above the imagination. After checking once, she locked the office door and found that her doubt was manageable and her anxiety much reduced. On walking to her car, she again had to reassure herself by reminding herself that the evidence from her senses, that is, the direct evidence from reality, was all she needed.

Following the above, she stayed late every second day and repeated the exercise. She found that she rapidly experienced fewer doubts and that they became less intense. She then decided to take a day's holiday to celebrate her success. The next week she started work on her OCD story about the home electrical appliances.

Ahmed

After practising his commonsense view on the doubt and the realistic view on the consequences if the doubt were true, Ahmed found that his level of belief in the doubt was still above 50%, and his anxiety about not doing the ritual still higher than 50%. He therefore went back to the steps in Chapter 5, and realized that there were some further elements in his OCD story ('yes ... buts') that he hadn't addressed in the commonsense view.

After some further work on the 'yes ... buts', his belief in the doubt went down to 45%. He thought about continuing this work but realized that he was starting to cover the same ground again and that he could come up with an endless number of remote possibilities for why the doubt was true. He therefore decided to proceed to facing the situation, and tackling his doubts and rituals after daytime driving trips using a graded approach. This is how he did it:

- Week 1: He stopped checking the sides and back of the car for blood and signs of a collision.
- Week 2: He stopped reading the newspaper.
- Week 3: He stopped checking the front of the car for blood or signs of a collision.
- Week 4: He stopped retracing his route.
- Week 5: He stopped checking his mirror when he went past a cyclist.
- Week 6 and thereafter: He focused on driving with care and sticking to the speed limit and using the steps for staying in reality when he had any obsessions. He started reading the newspaper again, but didn't pay special attention to reports of accidents.

Following this work on daytime driving, Ahmed started work on his OCD story and the commonsense view for night-time driving, which he had been avoiding since his OCD got worse.

Mark

Mark slowly found his belief in the doubt to be decreasing as he continued his written work on the OCD thoughts, but as he put it 'there were many hiccups'. For example, he'd read in the newspaper of an unexplained murder or a murder by a person with a mental health illness, or he'd watch a film about demon possession – material readily hoovered up by the OCD story as 'supporting evidence'. This required him to go back to the

OCD story a few times, add further information, and respond to it in the commonsense view. Finally, he felt ready to tackle the situation, with his belief in the doubt down to 35%, and his anxiety at 45%.

He opted for a graded approach using the following steps:

- He went into the garden shed and took out a small pair of pruning shears and put it on the table. Carole walked in holding the baby, and came progressively closer. As she approached, he experienced an increase in anxiety, and asked her to stand still until his anxiety reduced. Finally, she stood next to him and stayed there for 15–20 minutes until his anxiety had subsided completely.
- They repeated the above with the garden shears.
- On a different day, they repeated the same with an axe.

At this point, considering that Mark's work on the OCD story about the doubt in the garden shed applied equally to situations in the home, he repeated the above for doubts experienced in his home, for example, when holding the baby securely and standing next to the cutlery tray. As a result of this work, his confidence increased. He decided that the final piece of work would involve standing next to the baby holding a pair of scissors and actively holding the image in his mind of stabbing the baby. He reassured himself that the reality was that he had no intention of stabbing the baby; in fact, completely the opposite. He managed this situation with relative ease, knowing that all the evidence in reality pointed to the doubt being 100% imaginary and that there was no need to take it seriously.

Jenny

Jenny found that weeks of lengthy and thorough work on the commonsense view on the doubt, sometimes in consultation with her partner, almost eliminated any belief in the doubt. This went down to 5%. Following this improvement she had little difficulty, when noticing children and young people, not to feel that she had to scan her body for signs of sexual arousal. When she infrequently had obsessional doubts about the issue, they lacked intensity and she dismissed them by reminding herself of what she knew about herself from reality now and in the past.

The benefit from work on this doubt generalized to her doubts in other situations; for example, she was less concerned about her doubt about being sexually abnormal, when thinking the word 'sex' while taking care of her baby girl. However, she found that this continued to cause some upset, which is why she decided to devote some further work on her OCD thinking in this situation.

B. BEHAVIOURAL TRACK

8

Exposure and response
prevention therapy (ERP)

'Senri no michi mo ippo kara.' ('A thousand-ri journey begins
with a single step.')*

Japanese proverb

Chapter 2 provided you with an outline of a cognitive-behavioural understanding of OCD. You have seen how your decision whether to perform a ritual or avoid a situation depends on your thinking feeding into the obsessional doubt, which makes it seem very real, and your sense of which scary or unpleasant consequences might arise if the doubt were true and you didn't avoid the situation or perform the ritual. An option for proceeding with either the cognitive track (Chapters 5–7) or the behavioural track (Chapter 8) treatment was outlined. This chapter will describe the behavioural track option. This is an earlier but time-tested treatment for OCD called 'exposure and response prevention therapy' (ERP), which you may prefer if you already have a low level of belief in the obsessional doubt

* A ri is a traditional unit for measuring land in Japan.

and the feared consequences, and if you prefer this straightforward and direct approach.

So what does ERP entail and how does it work? As the name implies, ERP consists of two components:

- *exposure* – as opposed to avoidance or escape – to situations that trigger obsessions;
- *response prevention*, that is, not doing what you would normally do to set things right, reduce anxiety or discomfort, seek reassurance or escape feared consequences.

Exposure? Not ritualizing? I expect that you may consider these prospects with at least some trepidation, or at worst – shock and horror! A chill may be creeping slowly down your spine. Be reassured that this is a common and normal response in someone wrestling with OCD. But please do not despair, ERP is all about making the process as easy and within your reach as possible, even though it requires tolerating anxiety and discomfort – albeit temporarily – as a necessity. But first, how does ERP work?

How does ERP change my symptoms?

Think of the experience of jumping into a cold swimming pool. You steel yourself, tense your muscles, grit your teeth, tiptoe forward and jump. The cold water envelopes your body and ten thousand skin molecules cry out all at once: 'COLD!' But, as you stay in the pool, rapidly, after seconds or minutes, you get used to the water temperature and it becomes refreshing and invigorating.

Or, go to a jam jar and stick your fingers in the jam, thoroughly rubbing the jam all over both hands, then take them out again and just hold them, not cleaning. Listen to the radio for a few minutes. Most people would initially hold their hands up with their fingers spread out, but inevitably after a while they would relax and lower their hands as they become accustomed to having sticky fingers (i.e. you have 'habituated' to the sensation of stickiness).

These experiences illustrate one of the mechanisms that ERP harnesses for your benefit: the tendency towards 'habituation' or 'numbing out'. Psychologists define habituation as the decrease in the response to a 'stimulus' after repeated administration of the stimulus. In ERP this means that your level of anxiety or emotional discomfort, as a consequence of your obsessional fears, would tend to get less as you repeatedly expose yourself to the triggers of your obsessions.

You may counter by pointing out that you have had the obsession a thousand times and your anxiety has not got any less, or might even have got worse! This is a common experience and points to the obstacles that OCD cunningly puts in your way to prevent habituation from taking place. The most important obstacles are avoidance, ritualizing and reassurance-seeking. What they achieve is that your exposure to the trigger of your obsessions is not *of a sufficient duration or intensity* for habituation to be accomplished. For example, the anxiety caused by touching a contaminated object is eliminated by washing your hands and your partner reassuring you that the situation is safe, but this does not allow you a long enough period of time tolerating the anxiety to allow habituation to take place. In this way you prevent yourself from being 'deconditioned' to the anxiety or discomfort caused by the obsession about your hands being dirty. Furthermore, the use of rituals, avoidance and escape are 'negatively reinforced', that is, they are strengthened because they lead to a reduction in anxiety or prevent the experience of anxiety.

Therefore what is required for habituation or 'numbing out' to be accomplished is for exposure to be maintained for long enough and at a sufficient level of intensity (therefore allowing anxiety or discomfort first to go up and then go down), and to be conducted frequently enough (to allow the peak anxiety elicited during any single exposure to be reduced over the course of multiple exposures). That's why it is essential in ERP that a thorough, systematic and methodical approach is used, which includes exposure to the obsession *and* refraining from ritualizing or other ways of avoidance or escape. It is this rigorous approach that allows you to introduce the necessary structure in your ERP programme for making progress.

Traditionally, ERP emphasizes the importance of 'deconditioning' or habituation as described above. However, repeatedly exposing yourself to the feared situation without doing the ritual also allows you to realize two things:

• that your fears about the situation prove to be unfounded
• that you can cope with your anxiety or discomfort, which proves to be a *temporary* experience; it may be very unpleasant, but not dangerous – it first increases, then plateaus, and eventually gets less with repeated exposures (this is illustrated in the graph on Chapter 7, page 153).

Therefore in this respect ERP allows you to change your *thinking* about your obsessional fears.

How is ERP different from the cognitive track? In the cognitive track approach you first work on your obsessional thinking, leading to a reduction in your anxiety or other negative feelings, and then change your behaviour (i.e. face the situation and eliminate ritualizing). In ERP you change your behaviour in the situation, which results in a reduction in your anxiety and a change in your obsessional thinking.

Toolbox

Real-life ERP

Real-life ERP (also called *in vivo* ERP) involves confronting objects or situations that trigger your obsessions in real life, staying in the situation until discomfort subsides and refraining from attempts to protect yourself or others, setting things right by doing any other rituals or reassurance-seeking, or escaping or avoiding the situation in any way. Real-life ERP is particularly helpful where behavioural rituals (i.e. observable actions), rather than mental rituals, are the problem.

Examples of real-life ERP include the following:

- not washing your hands and handling your personal possessions after purposefully touching an object that triggers an obsessional doubt about contaminating your hands with germs;
- checking your gas cooker increasingly fewer times before leaving the house, until you finally check it once only;
- purposefully putting objects in the 'wrong' places or doing an activity in the 'wrong' order, if you have obsessions about the 'right position' or the 'right order';
- intentionally walking right past 'vulnerable' people, not on the other side of the road, if you fear that you might lose control and attack someone;
- attending church and sitting in the middle of the front pew if you worry that you might shout an obscenity;
- gradually reducing the time it takes to shave from 40 minutes to 10 minutes, if your ritual involves performing actions very slowly. (Further examples are provided below.)

Imaginal ERP

Sometimes it is not practically possible in real life to face the feared consequences associated with not performing rituals. In such cases repeatedly imagining the feared situation in vivid detail may be helpful, allowing your anxiety to the feared imagined scene first to increase, and then to become less as a consequence of repeated exposure. An example of imaginal ERP includes writing down in vivid detail what you imagine would happen if you accidentally knocked down a pedestrian, including witnessing the scene and giving a statement to the police, and then reading this passage over and over again until your anxiety gets less.

Alternatively, imagining exposing yourself to the situation and not doing the ritual (i.e. imagine yourself doing real-life ERP) may be helpful as preparation for facing the situation in real life in the way described previously. However, using imaginal exposure in this way should be preparation and not a substitute for real-life exposure.

Flooding versus graded ERP

'Flooding' is a treatment approach for anxiety that involves immersing yourself in the situation you fear most and staying in the situation until the anxiety gets less. In terms of the cold swimming pool analogy – it involves jumping in at the deep end and staying in, therefore involving *ungraded* exposure. However, the majority of people find an approach involving *graded* exposure more acceptable.

Graded exposure involves slowly walking into the pool one step at a time and getting used to (or 'acclimatizing to') every phase before proceeding. In the context of OCD that involves developing a *hierarchy* of obsession/anxiety-triggering situations in terms of their difficulty, and starting exposing yourself to 'easier' situations lower down in the hierarchy before moving on to confront more difficult situations. The main advantage of the graded approach is that it involves taking small steps at a time, thus breaking down the large goal of overcoming OCD into many smaller goals involving tackling one situation at a time. In this sense, it introduces the necessary structure into treatment to allow you to be more in control, thereby helping you to harness the confidence and motivation for moving forward.

Closed loop tapes

A closed loop tape is an audio recording device that allows continuous playback. This method is useful for treating obsessions where you mainly perform *mental* rituals (a mental ritual may involve purposefully thinking thoughts to 'undo' wrong, bad or unlucky thoughts – obsessions – which trigger anxiety). It involves describing and recording your obsession in some detail on a closed loop tape (or equivalent digital recording – many audio software programs allow repeat playback) and repeatedly listening to the recording – *while withholding yourself from performing the mental ritual.* Your anxiety will first go up, and then come down. Closed loop tapes are also useful in doing imaginal ERP (see above), where you record on the tape what you fear might happen, and then listen to the recording over and over again.

Treating yourself using ERP

The following sections will describe two phases. In the *assessment phase* you will first complete diary sheets to list comprehensively all the triggers for your obsessional fears. You will then arrange the trigger situations in a hierarchy according to how difficult it would be to face the situation while not performing rituals. In the *treatment phase* you will choose which situation to tackle first and then draw up and implement a detailed exposure plan for that situation. This will be repeated for each situation, moving your way up the hierarchy. Figure 8 illustrates the different steps.

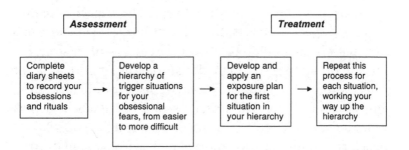

Figure 8 The different steps in ERP

Phase 1. Assessment

Our aim is to gain all the necessary information about your OCD symptoms and to organize this information in such a way as to make effective treatment possible. A useful initial step is to keep a diary of all the situations that provoke your need to perform rituals for one full day in the week and one day in the weekend. It is advisable to record details of the situation and of the ritual(s) performed – both behavioural and mental – and record the duration or number of rituals (diary sheets are provided in Appendix 4). This will allow you to record your rituals on the spot as far as possible, giving an idea how they feature in your daily life.

Following completion of the diary sheets, examine them carefully and write down the main situations/objects/thoughts/images that provoke obsessional fears on a piece of paper, including any which might not have arisen on the days for which you completed the diary sheets *and any situations that trigger your fears, which you avoid.* Group these together under different themes, for example, 'germ contamination', 'disgusting substances', 'attacking others', 'doing things in the wrong order', 'appliances being turned off', 'having bad thoughts', 'repeating actions', and so on.

Next, within each theme category, moving from item to item, consider what your level of anxiety or emotional discomfort is likely to be if you were to face the trigger situation (including specific objects, thoughts or images) *without doing any rituals.* Rate your level of discomfort on a 0–100% scale. It's only important to get a rough idea of your discomfort, so don't think too long about this. However, if you have difficulty rating your discomfort you could first assign a verbal label, such as minor/mild/moderate/severe discomfort, and then do a % rating. Generally minor discomfort would be from about 0–10%, mild would be from 10% to 30%, moderate would be from 30%

to 70% and severe would be >70%. Generally, we would expect situations requiring a greater number or more time-consuming rituals to elicit a higher level of discomfort if you didn't perform the rituals, although this may not always be the case.

The next step is to develop a hierarchy of trigger situations in terms of their difficulty within each theme category. This is a very important step as it provides the blueprint for how you will be progressing from tackling easier to more difficult situations. Using your emotional discomfort ratings for the situations above (including avoided situations) as an indication of difficulty level, rank the situations accordingly, from relatively 'easier' to more difficult (the first two columns of the 'Hierarchy of situations' worksheet in Appendix 4 may be used). Or you could rank according to the verbal labels you assigned previously (i.e. minor/mild/moderate/severe). Alternatively, if you find this too complicated, simply write down the situations on cards and rank the cards according to difficulty. Some people prefer doing the ranking by using the 'cut and paste' function on their computer.

Be careful that the OCD does not attempt to hamstring you at this early stage by rolling an obsessional doubt in your way, for example, 'Maybe I didn't do this in the right way' (and which you fear might cause the programme to fail) leading you to obsess about whether you ranked in the correct way or assigned the correct rating. This would simply be a part of the OCD problem, not a realistic concern. (In fact, beware of falling victim to these doubts arising at any point along the way). Remember there is no perfectly correct rank or rating – they are merely flexible signposts for your programme and can be changed if you reconsider your decision at a later stage or realize you missed or neglected an important issue. The point is to come up with a general outline covering the most important issues/situations allowing you to work efficiently towards achieving your goals.

Sarah

On the basis of the diary sheets she completed for a weekday and a weekend day, Sarah drew up a list of situations that triggered her 'germ obsessions'. She carefully thought about the rituals and safety strategies she used in each situation, and assigned a rating for her discomfort level if she envisaged acting in a normal way in the situation without performing rituals. On the basis of her discomfort ratings she arranged the situations in the hierarchy below.

Table 4 Theme category: Contamination by germs

Situation (describe the main situations/ thoughts/ objects or images that provoke your obsessional fears; rank the situations from easier to more difficult)	Discomfort (0–100%)	Tick when discomfort below 20%*
Using a public toilet	100	
Picking up an item from the floor in a public toilet	95	
Using a toilet in building where I work	80	
Picking up something from the floor in toilet of building where I work	75	
Shaking hands with a stranger	75	
Sitting on a train seat	65	
Sitting on a bus seat	65	
Touching door knobs in a public building	60	
Touching door knobs in building where I work	55	
Using someone else's telephone at work	55	
Using someone else's computer at work	50	
Sitting on someone else's chair	30	

* Use this column for tracking your progress with ERP

Richard

Richard completed his diary sheets and then developed a hierarchy for his obsessions about locking up (his work on 'bad' thoughts is described in the section, 'Using loop recording for treating mental rituals' – see below).

Table 5 Theme category: Situations where I have to lock up

Situation (describe the main situations/thoughts/objects or images that provoke your obsessional fears; rank the situations from easier to more difficult)	Discomfort (0–100%)	Tick when discomfort below 20%*
Locking up the house before going on holiday	100	
Locking up at home in the evening before bed	85	
Locking up at home in the morning before work	78	
Locking up the workshop before leaving at end of week (last person)	60	
Locking up the workshop at end of weekday (last person)	55	
Locking up my work area before leaving at end of week (not last person)	50	
Locking up my work area at end of weekday (not last person)	45	

* Use this column for tracking your progress with ERP

Phase 2. Treatment

The next section will give you an overview of how to use real-life ERP, which is appropriate for treating the majority of obsessions and rituals, followed by sections showing you when imaginal ERP and closed loop recordings may additionally be helpful.

Using real-life exposure

At this point you should have a hierarchy of situations (including objects, thoughts or images) that provoke your obsessional fears within each theme category, each with a discomfort rating from 0% to 100%. You are now ready to proceed to the treatment phase, with steps outlined separately for goal-setting and facing the situation.

Goal-setting

Step 1. Consider your hierarchy of situations. Decide which situation to tackle first. This involves drawing a compromise between tackling a situation that is not too daunting that the prospect of eliminating the ritual completely overwhelms you, and one that is difficult enough to allow you the opportunity of experiencing how your anxiety/discomfort first goes up, and then comes down again. My recommendation is to select a situation at about a 40–50% discomfort level. (If a situation does not elicit a sufficiently high emotional discomfort level, you won't be able to experience the benefits of habituation or 'numbing out' taking place.) Alternatively, you may prefer to start with a situation in which you *sometimes* succeed in resisting doing the ritual, and sometimes not.

Next, decide on a starting date for your programme. Also have an idea of when you would like to finish and aim to attain this goal, although your rate of progress will ultimately determine the duration of your programme, so be willing to be flexible.

Step 2. Develop an exposure plan for the situation you have selected to tackle first (the 'Exposure plan for one situation' worksheet is in Appendix 4). At this point your focus should shift away from the bigger picture of your OCD and hone in on the situation you will be working on, like a tennis player concentrating all their efforts on winning the point they're engaged in, and not allowing themselves to be distracted by thinking about the set or the match.

First you need to decide on a *behavioural goal*, which is how you envisage acting in the situation when OCD has walked off the stage and your action is based solely on reality and common sense, and your behaviour is similar to what one would expect of an average person acting reasonably and responsibly. When deciding on your goal, I strongly recommend against 'meeting the OCD half-way', that is, not eliminating *all* the ritualizing. If any rituals remain, this increases the chance of sliding back again, particularly when encountering stress in your life.

You may be unsure as to what appropriate behaviour is in the situation, and where ritualizing stops and normal behaviour starts. This tends to be the case where OCD has been walking in your shadow for a long time and where your obsessional thinking has muddied the water to such an extent that you find it very hard to trust yourself. If this applies to you, ask yourself what your common sense is telling you about the issue or how your behaviour was different before the onset of your OCD. Or you may choose to consult a trusted friend or relative, or observe what other people do. (I suggest conducting a mini-survey by consulting three trusted people on their behaviour in the situation – you won't get exactly the same answer from each, so average out what they say; for example, if one washes their hands after using the bathroom for 15 seconds, one for 20 seconds and one for 40 seconds, the average duration is about 25 seconds.)

To assist people with contamination obsessions, the Harvard psychologist, Dr Lee Baer, offers the following guidelines for washing: it's OK to wash after going to the bathroom; before eating; when seeing something dirty on your body; and when you touched something labelled poisonous (Baer, 2000). If you find yourself washing in different situations to those listed, ask yourself: 'Is it really necessary to wash?' Try to base your decision on the immediate reality of the situation that you perceive with your senses rather than vague scary possibilities. Also ask yourself how *important* it is to wash in situations where most people wash, and be careful not to think in extreme and catastrophic terms about what is likely to happen if you didn't wash in the recommended way (and this point also applies to any 'appropriate precautions' adopted as a behavioural goal in the situation, e.g. if you don't check after having used the oven, will it *definitely* catch fire?).

When asking people about their behaviour, be careful of the OCD shrewdly conning you into doubting that you have enough information, or that you don't understand the information adequately. Be content with the simple straight-forward method of enquiry and decision-making that charac-terizes the commonsensical approach. Resist the urge to ask for more and more information or seek reassurance. What may appear to be an unacceptable and even dangerous level of uncertainty is, in fact, just the OCD pulling the wool over your eyes. Allow yourself to be content with the level of knowledge that common sense or a reasonable approach requires, and resist the pulling power of the obsessional need for ever-elusive 'certainty' (a client described the experience to me as being like a small spaceship caught in the 'tractor beam' of a much larger ship). Instead reassure yourself that as you continue with your ERP work, the need for certainty will become less and less compelling.

Second, after deciding on your behavioural goal, you can plan to achieve this by doing ERP using a *single step*, that is, face the situation and eliminate the ritual in a single step. Or you may break the process down into a number of smaller steps, allowing you to increase your level of exposure and eliminate the ritual(s) using a *graded* approach, progressing from easier to more difficult steps. If you prefer a graded approach, when deciding on the different steps try to start at a level which will present a moderate challenge, but is not so difficult that you are likely to feel overwhelmed. (Whether you prefer a single-step or a graded approach, multiple repetitions of exposure sessions will generally be required to achieve a reduction in your discomfort – see later sections.)

It may be helpful to have an idea in mind of when you would like to have completed your exposure plan and move on to the next situation. When setting goals, be willing to push yourself, but also be realistic about the expected rate of progress. If you find that your progress is slower or faster than expected, be flexible and adjust your planning accordingly.

At this point, you might have got a sinking feeling in your stomach, as you contemplate what might seem the enormous challenge of ultimately stopping the ritual completely, even when using a graded method. You may not even be able to begin imagining yourself facing the horror of being in the situation without doing the ritual. However, fortunately there are ways of making this work easier. The secret lies in finding innovative ways of 'easing' yourself in the direction of finally eliminating the ritual completely, which should always be the final goal. American psychologists, Dr Edna Foa and Dr Reid Wilson, recommend the following strategies for making ritual elimination easier (Foa and Wilson, 2001):

- Postpone ritualizing. Progressively increase the duration of time before you perform the ritual, such as cleaning, checking or trying to reassure yourself. If all you can tolerate is waiting even just 30 seconds before you perform the ritual, that is still a good place to start. You are likely to find that as you wait progressively longer, the urge to ritualize becomes increasingly less.

- Change some aspect of your ritual. You may choose to change any of the following:

  ○ the *order* (if you start checking the plugs in one room and finish in another, change the order around; or if you allow yourself to use only the third tea bag you put in your cup, use only the second);

  ○ the *frequency* (if you do your action in three sets of fives, do them in two sets of sixes);

  ○ the *duration* (showering for 50 minutes instead of one hour);

  ○ the *objects* you use (wash with a different brand of soap);

  ○ *where* you ritualize (do one part of the ritual in one room, and another part in another room);

  ○ your *physical position or movement* during the ritual (instead of sitting when doing the ritual, stand up; or instead of keeping your eyes open, close them);

  ○ the *nature of the mental image* (if you bring a positive image to mind to neutralize the obsession, change the background in the image; say your lucky phrase in a different accent, such as American if you're British, or vice versa);

  ○ *participation of others* (if someone has to respond by saying a specific phrase, they could say a single word instead).

Drs Foa and Wilson point out that initially modifying your ritual in these ways has the benefit of making you more aware of how and when you perform rituals. By changing aspects of the ritual, you introduce flexibility, which is a bit like unpicking a few stitches in an item of clothing, ultimately causing it to unravel completely – you break the powerful magic of the ritual.

Facing the situation

At this point, you have selected a situation to start working on and developed a detailed exposure plan for that situation. You are now ready to do real-life ERP hands-on, tackling each step in your exposure plan when using a graded approach, or a single step when using a one-step approach, in the way described next:

Step 1. Using the first column of the 'Working on my negative thinking about exposure' worksheet in Appendix 4, write down your negative predictions ('hot thoughts') of what you fear might happen during and after exposure if you didn't perform the ritual. Also reflect on how you expect to feel during and after exposure, including how anxious you expect to be, and any fears you may have about losing control (which may be as bad as fearing that you will completely lose your sanity!). (See figure 7 in Chapter 7 on the experience of anxiety during ERP – people sometimes expect their anxiety to continue rocketing up, but in fact, during prolonged exposure, anxiety eventually comes down.)

Now, write down the commonsensical and realistic answers ('cool thoughts') to your anxious thoughts in the second column; for example, the fact that peak anxiety is a temporary experience and never continues indefinitely, and that high anxiety may be very unpleasant, but is not dangerous.

Be careful to limit how much time you spend on this part of the exercise. When spending excessive time, you might be playing into the hands of the OCD by procrastinating from facing the situation, or ritualizing in response to obsessional doubts, such as 'Did I do this in the right way?' or 'Do I have enough information yet?'

If you find that Step 1 is helpful for reducing anticipatory anxiety and helps you to engage with exposure, I recommend that you use it routinely during ERP. However, if you don't see a need for it, I suggest you proceed to Step 2 directly.

Step 2. Take a deep relaxing breath ... and face the situation that triggers your fears. This means exposing yourself *thoroughly* to the situation and facing your obsessions by *not protecting* yourself even by using subtle avoidance, such as not touching certain parts of an object, not sitting down on the bench fully, distracting yourself from the situation, imagining being elsewhere and so on.

Step 3. Withhold yourself from performing the ritual. This means *not using* any of the strategies that you would previously have used to make the situation safer or easier to tolerate, including behavioural rituals (e.g. cleaning, checking, ordering, asking for reassurance, repeating actions, performing actions very slowly) and mental rituals (e.g. 'cleaning' yourself mentally, counting, saying a prayer, thinking a lucky word or a lucky number). Rate your anxiety or emotional discomfort on a 0–100% scale at regular time intervals over the duration of the exercise, such as every 10 or 15 minutes (a worksheet is provided in Appendix 4: 'Tracking my discomfort'). You may also choose to chart your ratings on a graph with *Discomfort* (0–100%) on the vertical axis and *Time* (in 10- or 15-minute intervals) on the horizontal axis – it could be encouraging to see your progress illustrated graphically.

Step 4. Reflect on what you've learned about the effectiveness of exposure, your experience in the situation and the risks and dangers posed by the situation and complete the third column in the 'Working on my negative thinking about exposure' worksheet in Appendix 4 to record your insights. (*Steps 1 and 4 tend to benefit from doing written work.*)

Now continue practising your exposure by repeating steps 2 and 3 above, preferably on a daily basis, until there is a significant reduction in your discomfort (preferably until the peak discomfort elicited is below 20%), before moving on to the next step in your exposure plan. If you find this helpful, update your worksheets on your thinking before and after exposure (steps 1 and 4) as you learn more about the situation and your response to it with each repetition. Finally, when you've achieved your behavioural goal for the situation, move on to the next situation in your hierarchy of situations, develop an exposure plan for that situation, and repeat steps 1–4 above. It is a good idea to keep track of your progress by placing ticks in the third column of the 'Hierarchy of situations' worksheet as you overcome situations. This feedback is helpful for keeping up morale.

The following are the preconditions for doing real-life ERP successfully:

- Stay in the situation *long enough* to allow your anxiety to go up, then plateau and then start coming down (or habituate). It is better to allow continuous exposure rather than interrupted exposure, so try to schedule your exposure session in such a way as to avoid being interrupted. If you are interrupted and do not achieve anxiety/discomfort reduction, the exercise has not been used to its maximum potential. If this has been the case for whatever reason, try to carry on with the exercise after the interruption until you experience noticeable anxiety reduction.
- A rule of thumb is to grab the bull by the horns – *seek out the anxiety*, that is, while you are in the situation, go after the anxiety by doing things that increase your anxiety rather than the opposite.
- The power lies in the repetition. Perform exposure work on a daily basis or at least every second day, for at least 45 minutes per day, or even twice as long. Repetition is particularly crucial if exposure doesn't go according to plan, and you find yourself giving in to avoidance or performing a ritual. Continue the exposure exercises for a particular situation until your discomfort at its peak during the exercise has reduced to below 20%, and all ritualizing has been eliminated. Or at least carry on until there has been a significant reduction in your discomfort, allowing you to continue facing the situation without doing rituals in the course of everyday life.

- Try to avoid the situations higher up in your hierarchy when tackling a situation at a lower level. However, if this is not possible, perform the rituals you would have performed, but at least try not to exceed the level of ritualizing which you would normally have performed. When your discomfort in one situation has subsided and you tackle the next situation, it's essential that you continue *not to avoid* situations you have already worked on and continue not to perform rituals in those situations as you encounter them in the course of daily life. Also, continue not avoiding and not ritualizing in situations at a lower level of difficulty than those specifically included in your programme. Avoid at all costs 'compensating' for your ritual prevention work in one situation by increased ritualizing in another situation.

Sarah

When looking at her hierarchy of situations, Sarah felt quite daunted when thinking about the most difficult situation – using a public toilet. She sensibly opted to start working at the 'easier' end of her hierarchy and decided to start with the situation of using someone else's computer at work, which seemed at an appropriate difficulty level (the situation of sitting on other people's chairs, at a difficulty level of 30%, did not seem to present enough of a challenge).

She now focused all her attention on this situation. Reflecting on her thinking and behaviour in the situation prior to the onset of her OCD, she developed an exposure plan using a graded method, which included four steps for eliminating her rituals (see below). She discussed her final behavioural goal with Sean, wanting to know if he thought it was OK. When he replied in the affirmative, she checked with him again, and they discussed the fact that she already knew the answer to her question. They both agreed that this was a form of unhelpful reassurance seeking, and therefore part of the OCD.

Sarah's exposure plan for tackling the first situation

Table 6 Situation: Using someone else's computer at work

Hierarchy of steps for reducing ritualizing (rank the steps from easier to more difficult)	Tick when discomfort below 20%
Behavioural goal: Don't wipe down the keyboard before use; use computer for 45 minutes; handle personal objects; don't wash hands afterwards (except before eating or after I've used the toilet); normal physical contact with people and pets	
Wipe keyboard once before use using a tissue; use computer for 45 minutes; handle personal objects; don't wash hands for 60 minutes after use; normal physical contact with people and pets	
Wipe keyboard with antibacterial wipe once before use; use computer for 45 minutes; handle personal objects; don't wash hands for 30 minutes after use; normal physical contact with people and pets afterwards	
Wipe keyboard with antibacterial wipe once before use; use computer for 45 minutes; handle personal objects; don't wash hands for 15 minutes after use (never wash for longer than 15 seconds and use normal soap);normal physical contact with people and pets afterwards	

(Sarah carefully planned time in her diary for her exposure work at the office, allowing herself a break on the weekend.)
Another problem was what to tell my colleagues, because I was aiming to do the work at my office. This was an awkward prospect and I thought I'd test the water with my friend, Cate. She was very sympathetic but suggested I also have a word with our supervisor, Derek, and leave it

Continued

at that. I then explained to Derek what OCD was, and what was required for its treatment, and he was quite accommodating. We discussed the practicalities of my programme, such as which times of the day would be convenient for me to book to use the computer in the vacant office for my OCD work.

On the evening prior to my first exposure, I worked on my negative thoughts about the session. I spent a few minutes on completing the worksheet (see below), and this strengthened my resolve not to give in to the irrationality of the OCD. This, and doing some relaxation exercises, helped me to calm down a bit. A big part of it was just accepting the anxiety – I've dealt with worse in the past.

Table 7

What I fear may happen during and following exposure (write down your 'hot thoughts')	The realistic alternative (write down the 'cool', realistic answers to your hot thoughts)
I'll never be able to cope; my anxiety will just get worse and worse if I don't wash my hands immediately. Germs will be transferred onto my personal items, and I might get infected. Sean could be infected with a dangerous illness and get ill – like on holiday. The guinea pigs will get ill and might die, particularly the babies.	It's better to see if I cope and what happens to my level of anxiety, than just assume that the worst will happen – which there is every reason to expect that it won't. I'll try my best not to give in to the urge to wash immediately. Anxiety is a normal emotion that helps to protect us. It's uncomfortable but not dangerous. It's best to face the anxiety to increase my control over the situation and increase my confidence. My fears are exaggerated. People deal with this

Continued

situation every day in a routine way. They would have been worried if using other people's computers posed a real danger. Most people don't wash their hands even after they use computers in internet cafés. There is no realistic reason to expect the keyboard to be infected with dangerous germs.

On the next day when due to start my exposure, I thought of myself walking into the cold swimming pool, then sat down in front of the computer. I made sure that I was touching the computer properly, making sure that I tapped the keys as normal and used all my fingers. It felt really awkward and wrong, every single tap, and I felt my anxiety surge in anticipation of not washing my hands immediately afterwards, which just seemed like such a logical thing to do – I had to keep reminding myself that this was not the logical thing to do; OCD is not logical.

I managed to hang in there with the anxiety. It first went up to about 70% for what seemed like quite a while, in fact only a few minutes when I looked at my watch, then levelled off for 15 minutes or so at 50, and then to my great relief, started going down to about 20 at the end of 45 minutes. My anxiety went up again after I finished using the computer, and stayed high while I touched parts of my body and my personal belongings with my 'contaminated' hands, as planned. I thought of the germs on the hands of all the people who have used the computer before me and I had flashes of millions of grubby little germs crawling all over my body and being transferred to my personal belongings and spreading everywhere. But I reminded myself that the thoughts were symptoms of

Continued

> OCD, not facts, and after what seemed an eternity, finally washed my hands after 15 minutes.
>
> At home, my anxiety went back up to 60 as I handled objects and appliances in the house in the normal way and had constant worries about not having washed my hands immediately after using the computer. I fed the guinea-pigs in the usual way, and made sure I touched all of them, including the babies. Even in the state I was in, I couldn't help having a giggle thinking of how people were usually worried about being contaminated by small furry animals, not the other way around. Finally, towards the evening, my anxiety improved and it was about 10–20 at bedtime, which was a bit uncomfortable, but still manageable.
>
> The next day I looked at Sean – he seemed fit and healthy. The guinea-pigs were happily going about their guinea-pig business. Nothing happened. Everything was reassuringly routine. I spent a moment thinking about how this emphasized how my fears were without basis and completely unfounded, and how the OCD was conning me to take these fears seriously. I used the worksheet for recording that none of my catastrophic predictions came true and that the anxiety was more easily managed than I expected.

Sarah found her experience of her first exposure session very motivating and carried on with her exposure plan for the first situation. She found that repetition of exposure sessions was required for making adequate progress with each of the four steps in her plan before she finally achieved her behavioural goal, with her discomfort level below 20%. She placed a tick next to the situation on her 'Hierarchy of situations' worksheet, congratulated herself and felt encouraged by her progress.

Using the same approach as for the first situation, Sarah worked her way up the hierarchy of situations, one at a time. Sometimes she found a situation easier to tackle than she expected, and sometimes more difficult. On one occasion (when trying to pick up an object from the floor of the toilet at work), she found herself frozen with fear and had to go back to the drawing board and modify her exposure plan to include more steps in tackling this situation. She also asked her colleague, Cate, to assist her with the initial steps. In this way she managed to get her programme back on track again, by breaking big problems into their smaller parts and dealing with each in turn.

Some practical difficulties presented themselves as well – after initially being supportive, Sean was irritable on one or two occasions when she had to devote time to her programme, saying that she was already a lot better and could just as well spend more time enjoying life and going out on fun activities with him. Given that her progress had considerably eased the restrictions imposed by OCD on her life, Sarah was very tempted to bid the programme farewell and spend more time with Sean. Despite recognizing some 'permission-giving thoughts' such as 'my relationship is more important than my problems', she yielded to the temptation. But, some days later she found herself frustrated at the discomfort of needing to use the toilet because she was avoiding using a public toilet. Sensibly, she decided to continue and complete her programme. She rescheduled and after further hard work finally placed a tick next to the final situation (using a public toilet) two weeks later.

Staying on track

ERP involves actively *seeking out* discomfort – in order to reduce it and empower yourself. Therefore there is every reason to expect that flagging motivation, feeling dispirited and all the other stresses and challenges of everyday life may conspire to thwart your progress. It may be very tempting to procrastinate or simply throw in the towel and give up. Therefore to stay on track with your ERP programme, in addition to the specific guidelines for treatment outlined above, I suggest the following to sustain you along the way (it may also be helpful to read Chapter 4 again):

- Do your best to work consistently and methodically on your programme, and beware of the 'permission-giving' thoughts that might slow you down (e.g. 'I've had a hard day – I can't face up to my exposure work today'). Use the CBT strategies described in Chapter 4 to counter unhelpful ways of thinking. Be willing to examine carefully any reason for not doing or for delaying your exposure session and preferably change your plans only when there is a very good reason for doing so. Beware of using negative mood states as a reason for not doing exposure – your mood is likely to benefit from a sense of achievement *after* you have completed the exercise.

- Educate your family or other person who may be able and willing to help and support you in your ERP (they may benefit from reading Chapters 1, 2 and 8). Be quite clear to them about what they can do to help, but also be clear about what kind of support is *not* helpful, including any of the following:

  ° Any form of 'support' which assists in ritualizing, and which is in fact a part of the OCD (e.g. reassurance-seeking, such as whether a door is locked or an object is safe, or direct assistance in cleaning, checking or other rituals). This 'collaborative' ritualizing should be addressed as a matter of course in ERP, with the aim being a graded reduction in the amount of support provided.

  ° Any 'support' in doing ERP to make it easier, which in fact interferes in treatment (e.g. urging you to take a break from ERP when it would be better to get on with it, or interference with exposure in other ways).

- If resisting performing the ritual (e.g. repeating actions, or delaying checking or washing) is exceedingly difficult, the assistance of a helper may be invaluable. However, beware that the assistance provided is not counterproductive (see previous point). What you need is *moral and practical support*; for example, your helper showing an interest in your progress, encouraging you to face the situation, reminding you not to perform the ritual or disengage from ritualizing, being willing to suggest and engage in an activity to help distract you from ritualizing (such as going for a walk or engaging in conversation) and rubbing your neck and shoulders after a difficult session! (Your helper should never use force or ridicule you as a way of stopping rituals.) Ultimately, you should aim to face the situation under your own steam without assistance.

- If you find that you experience intense anxiety prior to or following exposure while you are resisting performing the ritual, you may find the relaxation techniques described in Appendix 5 helpful. This will not remove all the anxiety, but may take off the edge.

- Be creative in finding practical ways of helping yourself not to perform the ritual, particularly at the initial stage when the urge to ritualize is strong. For example, Dr Lee Baer (2000) recommends the use of the following strategy if your ritual involved rereading passages, which is based on a technique developed for teaching speed-reading: Point your index finger under the line you are reading and read as your finger moves across the page; when you get to the end of the line, move your finger to the next line and repeat the process. If you experience an urge to reread, keep on following the lead of your finger moving across the page and down to the next line. As you continue to practise this, the urge to reread should slowly subside. Use similar creative strategies to help you along the way with giving up other rituals.

- When you've managed to resist performing the ritual, reward yourself, for example, cook yourself a nice dinner or watch a good film. This helps to keep you motivated and not lose sight of the fact that every day presents an opportunity to win back time for yourself.

Troubleshooting

Problem: You're stuck – a situation is simply too daunting to contemplate exposing yourself to it.

Solution: Find ways of grading your exposure to the situation by using the strategies described previously. Even just choosing to change the ritual in a subtle way may pave the way towards reducing its power, spelling its eventual demise. It is almost always possible to find a way of starting at a lower level of difficulty. Even though this may require a longer timeframe for your programme, *anything – no matter how small – is better than nothing* (be heedful of Confucius: '*it does not matter how slowly you go so long as you do not stop*' – very true in this context). The important thing is always to keep on working within a trajectory where the arrow points to tackling more difficult situations in a stepwise progression.

Also remember that when you have experienced the benefits of ERP, it tends to get easier in respect of being familiar with the procedure and knowing what to expect, which is always easier than facing a completely novel situation. As you make progress with situations lower down on the hierarchy the ones higher up may become less daunting.

Finally, more intensive cognitive therapy work may be helpful for reducing anticipatory anxiety, if you are very fearful *before* your session (Step 1 under 'Facing the situation' above), or allow you to gain more from completed sessions, where you continue to be fearful *after* exposure (Step 4 under 'Facing the situation'). (Cognitive therapy methods are covered in more depth in 'Cognitive track' treatment in Chapters 5–7.) Work more comprehensively on developing a realistic perspective on the situation. However, *always be mindful of the danger of cognitive work evolving into ritualizing or procrastination*; at some point, when reasonably and commonsensically you have all the information you need, it is best to continue with the exposure work hands-on.

Problem: Due to external stresses or other mishaps your OCD surges and it is not possible to stick to your programme. You feel hopeless and conclude there is no point in trying further.

Solution: The road to recovery from mental health problems is almost always strewn with pebbles and rocks. In my years of treating OCD, examples of treatment programmes succeeding without a hitch are few and far between. Life is complex and unforeseen events occur. So, if things are not going according to plan, sound problem-solving is called for in the best spirit of the CBT approach. Think whether you need to take a holiday from the programme, and for how long. Consider whether, on the basis of new developments, you need to update your ERP programme to reflect any new symptoms that might have appeared or any worsening of existing symptoms. Pencil in a date in your diary for getting going again and stick to your plan!

Problem: You have repeatedly exposed yourself to a situation and not performed the ritual, and none of what you feared might happen has occurred, but your anxiety in the situation remains high.

Solution: You may also need to expose yourself to your *thoughts* about what you fear might happen in the situation. See the next section on imaginal exposure.

Using imaginal exposure

The goal of real-life exposure, as explained in the previous section, is to habituate to *feared situations in real life*. The goal of imaginal exposure is to habituate to your anxiety-provoking *thoughts*. Imaginal exposure is useful if you want to confront the catastrophes you fear may happen if you don't perform rituals (e.g. falling gravely ill after being contaminated); if the situations that you fear are difficult or impractical to recreate in real life (e.g. you fear being contaminated by being in a specific place which is difficult to access in real life); or if you want to prepare for real-life exposure through imagining being in the situation first (e.g. imagine handling an object that you fear might be contaminated). Follow the steps below.

Step 1. Write a passage, a few minutes long if you read it aloud, describing your experience when you face the situation *if you don't perform the ritual(s)* in as much detail as possible. Write in the first person and in the present tense. Describe what you fear will happen in the situation and your own thoughts and feelings. Describe the situation as vividly as possible, as you would describe a film from image to image. Try to describe your sensory experience – what you see, hear, smell, touch and so on. If you simply can't bear writing down all of your feared imaginings, first describe the situation up to a point that is bearable, say, with your emotional discomfort level at about 70%. Be careful not to insert in the passage any phrases to prevent the feared events from happening, such as 'God forbid this would happen to me'.

Step 2. Audio record the passage, reading it in the first person in an animated way – as if it was unfolding in front of you. For the sake of convenience, as you will need to listen to it repeatedly, it might make sense to use a closed loop tape or digital recording that allows repeat playback so you don't have to keep on rewinding a standard audio tape.

Step 3. Listen to the recording repeatedly for 45–90 minutes at a time. While listening, pay careful attention to what is being described, allowing your anxiety to go up (and eventually go down). The goal is to make certain that you feel distressed while listening to the recording. Rate your anxiety or emotional discomfort on a 0–100% scale at regular intervals, such as every 10–15 minutes, over the duration of the exercise. Continue your exposure session preferably until there is a noticeable reduction in your anxiety. Continue repeating your sessions until your anxiety at its peak drops below 20%.

If you previously left out details you couldn't face, now add these details to your passage, and follow steps 2 and 3 for the updated description until your anxiety subsides.

Richard

(Richard used a combination of real-life and imaginal exposure.)

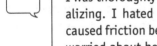

> I was thoroughly fed-up with my obsessions and all the ritu-alizing. I hated how much time they took and how they caused friction between me and Marie [Richard's wife]. I was worried about how it affected our relationship, and worried that things could break down. To show Marie that I was going to beat this problem, I asked her help with designing the programme. We decided on a real-life exposure approach, to do a thorough job of it. I felt impatient, but was aware that I needed to move slowly – if this could have been dealt with in an easy way, I would have dealt with it already, and this is clearly not the case.

When looking at his hierarchy of situations, Richard decided to start his programme by tackling the situation of locking up his work area at the end of a weekday, when he was not the last person to leave the workshop. He then *gave his full attention to his exposure plan for the first situation:*

> My behavioural goal was to check my cupboard, locker, equipment and window once only. This means looking at the window once to see if it's closed, and pulling once – gently – on the cupboard door and locker door to make sure it's locked. Scan around once, briefly (not more than 10 seconds) to check that all my equipment has been packed away. Nothing more and nothing less. No repeated checking, no repeated turning or pulling of handles, no checking from the side to see that the window handle is flat against the frame, no staring. I know that one check was all that was needed, and many people don't even check at all. I felt that I needed only one step for stopping the ritual in this situation.
>
> On Day 1, I made sure I was not the last person to leave the workshop. I finished packing up and locked up. I checked my cupboard, locker, workspace and window for a few seconds each, and once only. I tugged the cupboard and locker door handles briefly and gently. It was easier than expected. My anxiety went up to about 40%, a bit lower than I expected, and gradually went down as I walked away from the building, got into my car and drove away. By the time I went to bed that evening, I was completely at ease and I was no longer thinking about things being unlocked.

(Richard did not complete the worksheets for examining his anxious predictions before and after exposure, being convinced that his OCD thinking was 'daft and unreasonable', and proceeded directly to Step 2. He reflected afterwards that the session was easier than he expected and allowed him to feel more in control.)

Feeling confident and motivated, in the following days and weeks Richard steadily and methodically made progress. He worked his way up the hierarchy of situations, taking care to continue not to perform rituals when faced with situations lower down in the hierarchy, even when driven 'more by habit than worry'. By the third week, Richard felt that he had made sufficient progress with situations at work, to tackle his checking at home.

But his sessions on locking up at home in the morning before work turned out to be quite a bit harder than expected. Richard managed facing the situation and not performing the rituals on four occasions, but his anxiety did not get less in the way that he has come to expect on the basis of his previous exposure sessions and remained above 50% when he got to work in the morning. He found himself being plagued by thoughts about his house being burgled, valuable and sentimental possessions stolen, and the house being vandalized. He tried to banish thinking about the feared disasters from his mind. Sometimes he tried to reassure himself by substituting thoughts and images of the house being burgled and vandalized, with images of the house being locked and secure, but found that the former kept on pestering him.

After a few nervous days and a sleepless night, which was very unusual for him, Richard opted out of doing the exercise on the fifth day, feeling annoyed and disappointed with himself, the wind taken out of his sails. He gave himself a three-day break from his programme, and Marie reminded him of the progress he had made already, to encourage him. He reread his self-help materials and recognized that he had used a mental ritual (visualizing the house being locked and secure) to cope with his fear of the consequences if he didn't perform checking. He decided to prepare for further real-life ERP in his home by using imaginal ERP to confront the disasters he dreaded might happen if he didn't do his checking rituals. He updated his exposure plan for the situation of locking up at home in the morning, accordingly.

Following the steps for imaginal exposure described

previously, Richard drafted the following description of the feared consequences if he didn't perform his rituals:

It's ten past eight. I brush my teeth, pack my bag and smoke a last cigarette. I leave the house and walk to the car. Is everything locked and secure? I don't feel confident, but I decide to leave it. I drive away, get to work and start the day. Mike calls me over, looking worried, and says the police are on the line for me. I answer the phone. 'Is this Richard X?' I respond, 'Yes'. The policeman's voice is serious, as if I'm in trouble. 'I'm sorry to have to inform you there has been a burglary at your house; I suggest that you go there immediately.' I feel sick to my stomach, my heart is pounding. I rush down, get into the car and drive home. I can't bear to think what I'm about to see. I can see the flashing police lights as I approach the house. I can now see the house. A police car and van are parked outside.

Marie is already there, frowning and looking at me accusingly. A stern-faced copper walks over to me, saying that there was no sign of forced entry, someone left a door open. My knees go weak, I feel sick to my stomach. I walk into the house. Utter ruin, they took all the valuables and turned all the rest upside down. Everything that was locked has been forced open. The safe is empty. They urinated on the floor and on the furniture. Everything in the kitchen has been thrown out of its boxes. There is breakfast cereal all over the floor. A tap has been turned open with the sink closed and the living room carpet flooded. They trashed my collection of model planes, which I've been collecting since I was five years old. The only thing I can think is that I have messed up once again. I should have been more careful, checked more carefully. I was negligent. 'My negligence' – now the house is ruined, my worst nightmare come true.

In weeks to come, the insurance people tell me that because of the unforced entry, they're not paying out. I'm gutted but a solicitor tells me that it's in the fine print. I'm facing financial ruin.

Richard recorded the passage on a closed-loop tape and listened to it on his earphones for 45 minutes on three evenings. A few times he caught himself visualizing the house being locked and secure in an attempt to reduce his anxiety, and he had to shift his focus back to the tape. At the final session he found that his anxiety at its peak dropped well below 20%, and he found that he was starting to feel slightly bored listening to the recording. He then updated his planning and proceeded with real-life ERP the next morning. He found that the session was considerably easier than before he did the imaginal ERP, and his anxiety at its peak dropped below 50%.

The next day was easier and the rest of the next week easier still. Marie was particularly pleased when Richard no longer needed to ask her that everything was OK, doors locked, etc., after they went to bed in the evening (he included this as a specific goal in his programme). He continued in a similar way to work on situations higher up in the hierarchy, achieving his final goal of eliminating repeated checking when they went off on a family weekend away. This final step was difficult, but Richard found that a day after they arrived at their destination he had ceased to worry about the house not being locked up properly. The next trip was even easier.

Using loop recording for treating mental rituals

Loop recording represents a very useful way of exposing yourself to your obsessions when your rituals are mainly performed in your mind (mental rituals), and particularly if you tend to rely on coping through suppressing or avoiding the obsession. (Examples of mental rituals include repeatedly saying a short prayer to prevent a scary thought from coming true, neutralizing a blasphemous thought with a good thought, countering an unlucky number with a lucky one and so on.) In some ways mental ritualizing presents a bigger challenge for treatment than behavioural ritualizing, because the boundary between obsession and ritual is not as clear-cut and people have less control over their thinking than their behaviour. The following steps will help you to implement treatment.

Step 1. Buy a loop tape of the required length for recording your obsession or use digital recording allowing repeat playback. Now consider carefully which wording would be most appropriate for describing your obsession and write it down on a piece of paper. This may be very embarrassing or disturbing to you, but is a necessary stepping-stone for progress, so try to persevere!

If you have several disturbing obsessions, you could grade them according to how difficult it would be to face each one without performing rituals, and follow steps 1–2 for each in turn, working from easier to more difficult.

Distinguish the obsession from the ritual – the simplest way of making this distinction is to consider the obsession as being the initial thought(s) (which might include images or mental pictures) that *increase* your anxiety or other negative feelings. The ritual consists of the thoughts that you then harness to *relieve* your anxiety or reduce the discomfort triggered by the obsession or prevent feared events from happening. The obsession pops into your mind automatically, and you then initiate the ritualizing to 'deal' with the problem of the obsession.

Audio-record the obsession. (If you don't have a facility that allows continuous loop playback, simply record the obsession by reading it many times over on a conventional audiotape.)

Step 2. Listen to the obsession over and over again. Take care not to insert any thoughts to reduce your anxiety or discomfort while you are listening (e.g. telling yourself that it's only a tape or mentally distancing yourself from it) or any other rituals you would usually perform. All you need to do is to pay careful attention to the words being read. (An alternative to using audio-recording is to write down the obsession on a piece of paper and do exposure by reading it over and over again.) If you catch yourself starting to ritualize, simply refocus your attention on the obsession.

Rate your emotional discomfort on a 0–100% scale at regular time intervals (e.g. every 10 or 15 minutes). Continue listening preferably until your rating has dropped to below 20–30%. If you stop before this point, it is strongly recommended that you don't stop listening until there has been at least some reduction in your rating. After each exposure session, compare your predictions of what you feared might happen as a consequence of exposure with what actually happened, and reflect on what you've learned about the obsession. Repeat your exposure sessions until there is a meaningful reduction in your anxiety, for example, when your peak anxiety/discomfort is below 20%.

The point of these steps is to help you to coexist more comfortably with your upsetting obsessional thoughts, in part by proving that your fears about engaging with the obsession and not doing the ritual are unfounded (and this point also applies to real life and imaginal ERP). The focus is on accepting the obsessions more and resisting them less. The more you resist the obsessional thought, the deeper into trouble you will get yourself with OCD. The above exercises will help to remind you that the obsessions are only thoughts and do not represent a valid or realistic description, or allow valid predictions. It will start to dawn on you that your obsessional fears are unfounded. Armed with this knowledge, the best way of responding to the obsessional thoughts is of being an impartial observer, a bit like someone standing on a balcony watching people walk past on the pavement below, calmly at ease with the flow of pedestrians, not trying to control them.

Richard

You have previously met Richard and followed his progress in overcoming his checking compulsions. Following work on his checking, Richard proceeded to tackle his obsessions about his young daughter, Sue, using the steps described above.

> I felt really tense about it, ready to explode, but I managed to write down the worst thing I can think of: 'I hope Sue dies and burns in hell for ever.' After writing this down I had to neutralize the obsession, first by changing the bad words in the sentence to good ones, such as 'I hope Sue hides behind the bell' and then repeating 'God protect her' repeatedly, until it felt like the thought had been properly rubbed out. I then read the thought out aloud and recorded it on my loop tape. This again made me really uneasy, and I had to do my rituals again. I kept reminding myself 'no pain, no gain' – this was all a necessary step to getting better.

Richard then proceeded to Step 2, and decided to allocate half an hour a day before work for working on his obsession.

> It seemed this was the only quiet time in the house really, with Marie and Sue having left. Going to work would also get my mind off things, rather than it playing on my mind at bedtime.

When preparing for his first session Richard tried to reassure himself:

> I know that it's just a thought and there is nothing more to it, or in fact there was more to it – this was just OCD up to its tricks – causing unnecessary worry and hassle, but the only way I was going to get on top of this was to do my exposure and get my life back. That's why I decided to bite the bullet. I started listening to the tape, feeling very tense, but stayed with it. Another big problem was my mind constantly jumping to the ritual, but I kept focused on the words being read out. Just kept focusing, not distracting myself. At the end of 25 minutes of listening I decided to call it a day. My discomfort had gone down from 90% to 40%, so that was enough progress. Tomorrow was another day.

Continued

It was very difficult after the session not to do a ritual, and I worried about what might happen. I caught myself starting to do a ritual at various points, but then told myself to 'STOP!' and refocus on what I was doing, which worked OK. I had this nagging sense of disasters to come. But I reminded myself that a thought was all it was, nothing more, and I reminded myself that the vicar said this had nothing to with religion. When I got going at work it seemed to shift into the background, although I felt uneasy all day long. I didn't sleep well that night.

The next session (the following day) of listening to the tape was a lot easier, and my anxiety started at 60% and went down to 20%. Again, I had to fight against doing a ritual, and must admit one or two short rituals sneaked through, but I just refocused on the obsession. For the next three days I repeated the exercise and my anxiety at its peak went down to below 10%. At that point, and because absolutely nothing had happened – as I knew it wouldn't, Sue was 100% healthy and happy – I felt much less driven to do a ritual, yet had to keep my guard up and resist it on the odd occasion when I experienced an urge over the coming weeks.

Key points

- Exposure and response prevention therapy (ERP) involves prolonged and repeated exposure to triggers of your obsessions, *and* not performing rituals, escaping the situation or seeking reassurance from others.
- ERP works by promoting habituation or 'numbing out' as a consequence of repeated exposure, that is, reduction of the anxiety or emotional discomfort caused by your obsessions.
- In order to achieve habituation, exposure has to be of a sufficient duration and intensity, and conducted repeatedly. You have to seek out the anxiety or discomfort, not avoid or escape it.

- You also realize that your predictions about feared events don't come true, and that with prolonged exposure, your anxiety goes up, stabilizes and then comes down. You realize that anxiety may be very unpleasant, but not dangerous.
- Real-life ERP involves facing objects or situations that trigger your obsessions in real life.
- Imaginal ERP involves facing your anxiety-provoking thoughts.
- Graded ERP allows you to use strategies for grading the level of difficulty of situations you work on, moving from facing easier to more difficult situations.
- Closed-loop recording is a method allowing you to expose yourself to your obsessions and eliminate mental compulsions.
- Effective ERP requires you to work in a methodical way, by planning your programme carefully, keeping up morale and educating your family and others involved.

PART THREE
STAYING WELL

9

Using a holistic approach

An unfortunate thing about this world is that good habits are much easier to give up than bad ones.

W. Somerset Maugham

Pursuing meaning in your life

The Austrian psychiatrist Viktor Frankl (1905–1997) said that humans' main motivation for living is to find meaning in life, and that life offers us meaning in all circumstances, even the most miserable ones. We always have the freedom to decide on the attitude we take towards events in our lives, and so find meaning in them. Discontentedness and emotional disorder are the consequences of losing sight of positive meanings in our lives. Frankl should know about these things. He survived the Nazi concentration camps during the Second World War, where he lost his parents and his wife, and he developed his theories on the basis of these experiences.

But how can these perspectives help you in coping with your OCD? First, it may be helpful to think of what a positive meaning entails. My view is that this refers to those experiences in our lives that support *lasting* contentedness and give us a sense of purpose. In this sense, it excludes activities such as materialistic pursuit of acquiring possessions, or alcohol or substance abuse, as these activities will usually only lead to a short-lived and superficial elevation in well-being. This is usually followed by a slump, feelings of emptiness and an ever-increasing craving for more.

Therefore, if positive meanings are important as Frankl contends, it may be helpful to think about the balance of positive and negative meanings in your life, and how this may have been shifted in a negative direction by your OCD. If you make it your goal to use cognitive-behavioural therapy (CBT) to change this balance in a positive direction, considering the following may be helpful to you:

You have lost sight of the positive meanings that already exist in your life

As we have seen in Chapter 2, CBT encourages us to examine our thoughts about ourselves and our lives, and to correct misconceptions based on inaccurate thinking. It may be that OCD has increasingly started to take centre stage in your life, leading to the rest of your life being obscured. In this way it may have caused you to devalue or ignore what is good and right in your life, and this distorted perception can only serve to strengthen the OCD's hold on you by leading you to feel discontented and frustrated. If this is the case, now is the time to rethink.

One way of trying to correct this skewed perception is by doing the following simple exercise – try to remind yourself of the positive meanings that exist in your life, in an *inclusive* way. This is easier said than done, which is good reason to spend time on this exercise, putting pen to paper. Be very wary of negative thinking distortions creeping in (see Chapter 2). You may choose to think of the following:

- Good experiences in the present and the past. Remember that having OCD does not *undo* good experiences now and in the past. Good will always be good. You can already give yourself credit for tackling the OCD by reading this book. Be wary of *depressive memory recall bias*, that is, because you may be feeling low, you may have a tendency to remember negative past events to the exclusion of positive events.

- Your relationships. Write down the positives that *are there*, not the positives that are missing, or the negatives. Think of people whom you care about and recognize that the fact that you care about them is a positive. Think of the qualities you value in them and the qualities they value in you. Recognize that nobody is perfect, and appreciate that some dark clouds may have silver linings; for example, your boss may have a temper and occasionally be grumpy, but she did a sterling job of sorting out the problems you had with that pesky IT person not giving you what you needed!

- Small things. These are easily taken for granted. Try to remember people who showed kindness to you, even just a smile, or a small courtesy. Think of what you offer others, and again recognize the small things – letting another driver turn into the road ahead of you, giving a small amount to a person with a charity tin, having a kind thought about somebody, or doing a job well. Each one of these small things is a positive meaning and should be recognized as such.

- Humour. A humorous perspective, devoid of malice, presents an excellent strategy for instantly changing your perspective on things, including yourself. Be willing to use it. Research studies have shown that the use of humour as a stress-coping strategy has benefits for mood and the immune system.

Increasing positive meanings and reducing negative meanings

The above section is about becoming aware of what is already there. This section is about grabbing the bull by the horns – actively addressing the problem of too few positive meanings and too many negative meanings in your life. Consider the following:

- Improve your relationships and invest in new relationships. Human beings are inherently social. That's why it would be difficult for anybody to be impervious to the state of his or her relationships with other people. And that's why it is a good idea to deal with problems in your relationships on an ongoing basis. The purpose of this book is not to provide detailed relationship advice (which can be found in *Love is Never Enough*, 1988, written by a pioneer of cognitive therapy, Dr Aaron Beck), but the following are a few things to think about:
  - ° Try to communicate clearly, honestly, directly and with sensitivity.
  - ° Find a 50–50 balance in conversation between telling people things and listening to them.
  - ° Be interested in people, ask them questions and listen to their replies.
  - ° Be fair – acknowledge when you've made a mistake.
  - ° Be neither the dragon (aggressive), nor the doormat (overly submissive), but assertive. This means standing up for your rights in a way which is calm and respectful of the other person.
  - ° When complaining, try to present the other person with a solvable problem, and suggest a practical solution.
  - ° Criticize the behaviour, not the person.
  - ° Be prepared to take risks by reaching out to others.
  - ° Accept that investment in a new relationship may not immediately bear fruit.

- Deal with practical problems effectively and efficiently – this usually involves a careful and methodical approach to defining the problem, weighing up ways of addressing it, implementing a solution and evaluating the consequences. Work on developing habits that increase your efficiency. For example, get into the habit of putting pen to paper. Make lists of things to do and tick them as you go along. Invest in keeping your home and working environments neat and organized (what does your environment signal to you about yourself when you open the door?). Pick the task that you least like to do first, and reward yourself when you've completed it.

- If you're unemployed, or on extended sick leave, perhaps because of your OCD problems, try your best to reconnect as quickly as possible with the mainstream of employed life. The longer you delay this, the more difficult it tends to be. Remember the practical benefits of work: it pays you a wage, it helps to structure your day and it focuses your attention on tasks removed from your mental health concerns. If salaried work is not an option, consider doing voluntary work or a work experience placement, which may sometimes allow you to progress to a salaried position. If there are problems in your work other than as a consequence of OCD, try to deal with these in as practical and efficient a way as possible.

- An American psychologist, Dr Cory Newman, believes we should 'create more, consume less'. Many people have the experience of investment in creative activities ultimately being more rewarding than mere consumption of goods – 'creative therapy' tends to work better than retail therapy! Try out new activities or start again with ones that you have stopped doing – join an art class, take a cooking course, take up woodwork or tackle some DIY, try creative writing, start gardening, perfect that drop shot when playing squash or tennis, or try yoga or kick-boxing. Be careful of falling victim to 'affluenza', defined as 'The bloated, sluggish and unfulfilled feeling that results from efforts to keep up with the Joneses'! (Public Broadcasting Service website: www.pbs.org/kcts/affluenza/)

- Invest in acts of kindness to others and causes bigger than yourself (be a 'go-getter' and a 'go-giver'). Research shows that people who practise altruistic behaviour tend to be happier – that means the kindness may also benefit the giver!

- Develop your spirituality. This involves reminding yourself of the meaning of your existence in the context of your life and the world. Many people derive sustenance from their religious beliefs in dealing with the challenges and calamities that life throws in their way. If your OCD has caused you to cease participating in your church, or other institution of faith, consider attending again and reconnecting with members of your religious community. If you are not religious, examine the non-material things that are meaningful to you in life, whether this is the inspiration of poetry, the sense of transcendence that music can offer or quiet moments in tranquil surroundings.

- Take time out of the rat-race. Carve out space in the day that is just for you, whether this is first thing in the morning, or a lunch break where you actually leave your desk, or a space at the weekend where you are completely alone and do nothing at all.

- Spend more time in nature. The beauty of nature has inspired poets and artists for millennia – you can benefit too.

Is it possible to find a positive meaning in your experience of OCD?

Viktor Frankl would consider this question the biggest challenge of all – how to find meaning in distress and suffering? However, if you examine your experience very carefully, some positive meanings may emerge. For example, perhaps you have had off-putting experiences with people who are negatively prejudiced against those who suffer from mental health problems. Frequently, such prejudice is founded in ignorance – a lack of understanding of the experience of mental health problems. Being clinically depressed isn't the same as feeling a bit low, and you can't 'just snap out of' doing your rituals.

Given the nasty consequences of ignorance about mental health conditions, consider how much less ignorant you are now because of your experience of OCD or because of reading this book. This understanding allows you to have more compassion and to be kinder towards others who suffer from mental health conditions. This benefits them, and as we have seen above, also benefits you. You emerge the wiser person.

Exercise and a healthy lifestyle

> Fresh air impoverishes the doctor.
>
> (Danish proverb)

Most people would accept that our mind is related to our brain. However, surprisingly, the mind is often considered to be quite separate from the body. This view is sometimes challenged by the experience of physical illness, like a bad cold, when we suddenly realize how miserable we may feel when our body is in the throes of viral attack. This dramatically brings home the truth that mind and body are one. Your mind depends on your brain, which depends on your body.

It follows that your brain and your mind will benefit if you treat your body well, and this becomes particularly important when you are struggling with mental health difficulties. This emphasizes the benefits of taking care of your body for tackling OCD or other mental health problems, like depression or anxiety. There are three key ways of taking care of your body: regular exercise; a healthy diet; and the regular practice of relaxation.

Regular exercise

Over and above the considerable physical benefits, the following are the psychological benefits of exercise as proven by research studies:

- Reduction of worry and anxiety.
- Reduction of symptoms of depression.
- Improved quality of sleep.
- Improved self-confidence and body image.

In fact, several studies have found that regular exercise of moderate intensity is as effective as other treatments for mild to moderate depression. This has recently led to a major initiative in the UK to enable GPs to refer their patients with depression for exercise training.

Further, there is now evidence that exercise may even have a direct benefit in OCD. In an American study, conducted by Dr Richard Brown and colleagues (Brown et al., 2007), 15 people with OCD who had been having treatment with medication and/or CBT for at least three months, participated in a moderate-intensity aerobic exercise programme for 12 weeks. The programme entailed exercising initially for 20 minutes increasing to 40 minutes three to four times a week, and just less than half the group continued to exercise on their own six months after the programme had ended. Reductions in OCD symptom severity at the end of the exercise programme, and six months after the programme, suggest that exercise in itself may benefit OCD symptoms. However, it is not possible to reach a firm conclusion yet, because the study did not include a comparison group who did not exercise at all.

But how does exercise benefit the mind? Many different mechanisms may be responsible, but researchers have found that exercise providing a significant physical challenge causes changes in the brain, such as in levels of feel-good chemicals like endorphins and serotonin. Muscles feel more relaxed after an exercise session, which may promote relaxation and feelings of well-being. These benefits are of great help when you are tackling a formidable opponent like OCD.

HOW MUCH DO I NEED TO DO?

Experts recommend that to benefit your health, you need to be physically active at mild to moderate intensity for 30 minutes on at least five days of a week. That may sound like a lot, but remember that this doesn't need to be strenuous exercise – it could be as little or as much as a brisk walk during your lunch hour or a series of yoga stretches in the morning. If you want to get properly fit, you may of course choose to do more strenuous exercise. The golden rule is to build your fitness up gradually. Naturally, these recommendations will be different if you suffer from a physical health problem, so consult your GP if you have questions about health and exercise.

WHAT HAPPENS NEXT?

If you're currently inactive, or feel that you would like to do exercise in a more consistent or structured way, make it a project to look at what is on offer. Make an appointment with your local gym and look around, or ask for advice at your GP surgery. Community centres frequently have notice boards advertising exercise classes.

If you have a very hectic schedule, try to build exercise seamlessly into your day. For example, get off the bus or train one stop before your place of work, park in the furthest space in the supermarket parking area, or use the stairs instead of the lift. Every little helps.

Try to introduce a gradual, but self-sustaining change in your exercise routine rather than opting for sudden fireworks, which are frequently short-lived (gyms are usually much busier in the first weeks of January than later in the year). Do this by making your exercise stimulating, structured and as enjoyable as possible. This may include using an iPod in the gym or going for a walk in the park rather than around the block. Again, if you have a hectic schedule, pencil in time for exercise. Work on low motivation and unhelpful thinking, such as when you feel self-conscious in the gym or a group setting, by using the strategies described in Chapter 4.

Be careful to demand that exercise *always* be enjoyable, or that it should be immediately rewarding – many people enjoy exercise more the fitter they get. Also be careful to be fooled into not doing exercise by depressive tiredness, as opposed to normal tiredness, which tends to improve in response to increased activity.

A healthy diet

Did somebody ever tell you that you are what you eat? Well, it's true, and it's important for all people to recognize this, particularly those who suffer from physical or mental health conditions. Findings from research studies are increasingly suggesting that your physical health and mental health benefit from following a healthy diet.

What's more, following a healthy diet *now* may well benefit your mental health *in future* by helping you to avoid conditions such as cancer, heart disease, stroke or diabetes. Detailed guides are found elsewhere, but the following are basic recommendations:

- Have at least five portions of fruit or vegetables a day (these contain micronutrients, including *antioxidants*, that mop up harmful unstable particles called *free radicals* in the body and in the brain).

- Have as little saturated fat as possible (sources of saturated fat are fatty red meat, cheese, full-cream milk, butter).
- Use unsaturated fats instead (sources include olive oil, sunflower oil, rapeseed oil, fish oil – where possible, have cold-pressed oils, which are healthier).
- Opt for whole foods rather than refined foods (e.g. brown bread rather than white bread).
- Eat one or two portions of fatty fish every week, such as tuna, sardines or salmon.
- Drink about six to eight glasses of water a day.
- Limit sugar, salt and caffeine.
- Don't overdo alcohol (men shouldn't have more than 21 units of alcohol in the week, and women 14; a small glass of wine or half a pint of ordinary strength beer is about one unit).

With specific reference to the brain, in a review article in a prestigious scientific journal, Dr Gómez-Pinilla, of UCLA, discusses the potential importance of omega 3 fatty acids (found in fatty fish and flax seeds), antioxidants (high levels in berries) and folic acid (spinach and orange juice) in supporting good mood and intellectual abilities (Gómez-Pinilla, 2008).

HOW DO I DO THIS?

If you suspect that your diet isn't as healthy as you'd like, follow these steps:

- Record your food and fluid intake over the course of one day in the week and the weekend.
- Identify what you need to change by comparing your diet with the guidelines above.
- Develop a programme for substituting problem foods with healthy ones, outlining when what is going to change.
- Implement your programme and monitor your progress.

When you develop your programme for healthy eating, be realistic and allow yourself one or two vices, but make sure that the balance lies on the positive side – the impact on your health is the end result of all the foods included in your diet. As with any change in behaviour, you may find that old habits die hard. However, remind yourself that when your new healthy habits have become established (e.g. once you've learned how to cook tasty meals using healthy ingredients), things will be much easier. The BBC website provides further advice on changing your diet.

Progressive relaxation

Progressive relaxation therapy (PR) is aimed at reducing levels of general muscular tension. I was initially dubious about the virtues of this technique, but after I participated in a session led by a colleague and almost fell asleep (unusual for an insomnia sufferer!), I became a convert. You will find the steps described in Appendix 5. I suggest that you practise these at least once daily to reduce your general levels of anxiety and tension (particularly important in the context of dealing with OCD), which may also be useful for helping with insomnia. Remember – PR is a skill, the more you practise the better you'll get. Do not expect to play tennis the first time you pick up a racquet! If you prefer a more hands-on approach (literally), consider getting a regular back massage from an accredited therapist, which does wonders for resolving the effects of stress on the body. The resulting feelings of physical well-being will do a good job of arguing against stress-promoting negative thoughts – it is now recognized that the mind is also influenced in its interpretations of the world by the signals it receives from the body.

Key points

- A positive meaning is an experience that supports lasting contentedness and gives a sense of purpose.

- OCD may reduce the positive meanings in your life and increase the negative meanings.
- Address this imbalance by reminding yourself of positive meanings that exist already in your life, or by actively introducing new ones.
- Positive meanings may be created by improving your relationships, adopting useful roles, being kind to others and doing more creative activities.
- Reduce negative meanings by working on problems more effectively.
- The experience of OCD can make you a wiser and more sympathetic person.
- Your body and your mind are connected.
- Benefit your mind by treating your body well – do regular exercise, practise relaxation and follow a healthy diet.

10

Taking stock and staying well

The previous chapters presented self-treatment approaches focused either on correcting the faulty thinking underlying your obsessions and rituals (cognitive track), or on targeting your avoiding and ritualizing directly (behavioural track). Chapter 9 dealt with holistic issues in the treatment of OCD.

If you have been working on the exercises as you go along, I hope you have made progress to the point where your obsessions have ceased troubling you, and you no longer see the need to perform rituals or avoid situations that trigger your obsessions. The first part of this chapter will consider how to stay well if you have made satisfactory progress with your OCD. The second part will consider what to do next if you feel that more needs to be done.

Dealing with obsessions and rituals if they recur

Well done, you've worked hard and I assume that you've made significant progress. Your new ways of thinking and acting have established themselves in those areas in which the obsessions and rituals previously reigned supreme. However, OCD has a tendency to pop up again when you least need it – when you're stressed out or feeling low, or are anxious because of life changes or other problems.

You may wonder how this is possible if you've managed to overcome your current obsessional problems. Surely the problem is done and dusted?

The psychological explanation for the risk of relapse in OCD is that once new beliefs and ways of thinking and acting have established themselves, the remnants of the old ones are not completely eliminated. It's like ancient ruins continuing to exist underneath the foundations of a new building. Therefore there continues to be a risk that the OCD thinking tendencies may resurface in similar ways or in different areas.

This may seem a scary prospect, but remind yourself that at such a time you will have a major advantage – knowledge and experience. You will know that OCD, rather than being a towering giant, is in fact a shifty charlatan. Now that you know his tricks, he will be much easier to face down if he comes around again. In this respect, if you re-experience obsessional doubts at any point or find yourself tempted to perform rituals, simply follow the steps in the relevant chapters, depending on your preference for cognitive or behavioural track treatment. A good straightforward way of preventing obsessions or rituals from gaining a foothold is to refrain from doing any form of ritual right from the start and not avoiding situations that trigger obsessions.

Try not to be disheartened if you experience obsessions again – this is not a sign of weakness, but is simply a reminder that, as with a multitude of things in life, you have to keep on working to keep on improving.

Reducing the chances of relapse

The previous paragraphs concerned direct ways of addressing obsessions and rituals if they resurface. However, this still leaves an important issue unaddressed – how to prevent the conditions that increase the likelihood of relapse from arising in the first place. These conditions are chronic, elevated stress and low well-being – fertile soil for OCD and other mental health problems. I suggest the following ways of keeping your mental health in shape.

Developing your cognitive-behavioural therapy (CBT) skills

The journey to rational living is a lifelong quest. This may sound trite, but is true. It is vitally important that you continue to hone your skills of stepping back from the negative thoughts you have about yourself, other people, situations or issues; considering how realistic or accurate your thoughts are; and reflecting on alternative, more balanced and more objective ways of thinking. Alternatively, teach yourself the methods of mindfulness-based cognitive therapy, and practise these regularly (as described in *The Mindful Way through Depression*, by Mark Williams and colleagues). In this way you will continue to avoid or reduce the experience of unnecessary low mood, anxiety and upset.

Dealing actively with life problems

You may have had the experience that making inroads with your OCD has made you aware of other problems that were previously obscured by the OCD; this can be a bit like finding smaller weeds when the bigger weeds have been pulled out. Make it a habit to deal *actively* with such problems, and problems that may present themselves in the future. Ongoing problems are frequently camouflaged villains affecting your outlook – you may not be aware of how they subtly bias your perceptions in a negative direction. So, if you have financial problems, cut costs and try to increase income now, and make an appointment for expert advice next week. If the grass needs cutting, get on with it this weekend. If your boss has been driving you mad, make an appointment to see him today. If you need a break, grab your diary and get on to that travel website!

Maintaining a healthy lifestyle

The virtues of a healthy lifestyle – regular exercise, a healthy diet and practising relaxation – have been described before. These are particularly helpful when working on your OCD, but are even more helpful in reducing the risk of relapse by helping you to maintain good physical and mental well-being, generally, and taking the edge off stress. Make it a lifelong project.

What to do if you feel that you need more help

I hope that reading this book has been helpful to you. However, you may have found that you have not made as much progress with your OCD as you would have liked and that more needs to be done. Please do not feel disheartened. If you tried either cognitive or behavioural track treatment, and your progress has been unsatisfactory, it may be worth trying the other approach. Alternatively, you may consider getting assistance from a therapist or using medication. Even if you have tried these before, without the desired effect, remember that there is the possibility of working more effectively with a different therapist or trying a different medication. In respect of pursuing either option, I refer you to the relevant sections in Chapters 1 and 2. Appendix 1 provides a list of useful resources for OCD if you feel that you need more information or support.

A last word of encouragement

I sincerely hope that the ideas put forward in this book have been of benefit to you and that the progress of Sonya, Andrew, Clare, Ahmed, Mark, Jenny, Sarah and Richard serves as encouragement. A final word: if you have tried, and not succeeded, keep on trying – Rome wasn't built in a day!

Key points

- There is a risk that your obsessional doubts and rituals may recur.
- If this happens, you will have the benefit of knowledge and previous experience.
- Reduce your chances of relapse by managing your stress by developing your CBT skills, dealing actively with problems and maintaining a healthy lifestyle.
- Deal with obsessional doubts by using the methods described previously in the book and refraining from performing rituals right from the start.

Appendix 1

General resources

The following national organizations offer support to those suffering from OCD, including news updates on new research and treatments, and information on self-help groups and referrals to mental health professionals and services.

UK

OCD-UK PO Box 8955, Nottingham NG10 9AU
    Email: admin@ocduk.org
    Website: www.ocduk.org
OCD Action Davina House, Suites 506–507, 137–149 Goswell
    Road, London EC1V 7ET
    Help and Information Line: 0845 390 6232
    Telephone/fax: 0870 360 6232
    Email: info@ocdaction.org.uk
    Website: www.ocdaction.org.uk

USA

The Obsessive Compulsive Foundation PO Box 961029,
Boston, MA 02196
Telephone: (617) 973 5801
Fax: (617) 973 5803
Email: info@ocfoundation.org
Website: www.ocfoundation.org

The Anxiety Disorders Association of America 8730 Georgia
Ave., Suite 600 Silver Spring, MD 20910
Telephone: (240) 485 1001 Fax: (240) 485 1035
Website: www.adaa.org

Canada

Mood Disorders Society of Canada 3–304 Stone Road West,
Suite 736 Guelph, ON, N1G 4W4
Telephone: 519 824 5565 Fax: 519 824 9569
Email: info@mooddisorderscanada.ca
Website: www.mooddisorderscanada.ca

Appendix 2

Thought recording form*

* Please refer to Chapter 4

Thought recording form: instructions*

Date	Situation	Emotion/ feelings	Automatic thoughts (the 'hot thoughts')	Rational alternative perspective (the 'cool thoughts')
	Describe: 1. Actual event leading to negative feelings; or 2. Fantasy, daydream, image or memory of an event leading to negative feelings.	Specify sad/ anxious/angry/ frustrated/ depressed, etc. Rate on a 0–100% scale.	Write down the automatic thoughts (or mental images) that preceded the negative feelings. Ask yourself: what was going through my mind? Try to be as specific as possible.	Ask yourself if there could be a more realistic, fairer way of looking at the situation. Are you ignoring or negatively distorting important information (e.g. catastrophizing/all-or-nothing thinking)? How would a scientist look at the situation? What would you say to a friend having these same automatic thoughts in a similar situation? Answer your 'hot thoughts' with this 'cooler' *more balanced* perspective – is there a corresponding change in your feelings? If so, rate the % change (e.g. 10% reduction in anger). Now, what can you do to improve the situation?

* Different versions of thought recording forms are available, among them that published by the Beck Institute for use by therapists (Beck, 1996).

Thought recording form

Date	Situation	Emotion/ feelings	Automatic thoughts (the 'hot thoughts')	Rational alternative perspective (the 'cool thoughts')

Appendix 3

Cognitive track worksheets*

---

* Please refer to Chapters 5 and 6

Obsessional doubt worksheet: instructions

Date: _____*Trigger*: _____

Obsessional doubt: (Ask yourself: what is *not OK* in the situation? What is it I have to be 100% sure of *not* to have to perform the ritual?)

_____

OCD story	Commonsense view
Ask yourself: why may this doubt be *true* or a *real possibility* and what is the argument supporting the doubt? Write down all you can think of. Keep on adding to the list as you think of more reasons. Rate how much you believe the doubt on a 0–100% scale.	Now reflect on the OCD thinking devices used in the OCD story. Ask yourself: what do my *senses* tell me or what have my senses told me about the doubt? What does *common sense* tell me about the doubt? Try to answer all the points made in the OCD story. If any 'yes ... buts' come up when you think of commonsense points, add them to the OCD story and then answer them below. Re-rate how much you believe the doubt on a 0–100% scale.

Obsessional doubt worksheet

Date: _____ *Trigger:* _____

Obsessional doubt:

_____

_____

OCD story	*Commonsense view*

Feared consequences worksheet: instructions

Date: _____

Obsessional doubt: (Ask yourself: what is *not OK* in the situation? What is it I have to be 100% sure of *not* to have to perform the ritual?)

_____

Current view	Realistic view
Ask yourself: what would happen if the doubt were true and you did not perform the ritual/avoid the situation? How likely is that to happen? How would you cope? How would others affected cope? How much would you be to blame? What would it mean about you as a person if the worst happened? Rate your level of fear about the consequences on a 0–100% scale.	Ask yourself: what do *reality* and *common sense* say about the likelihood that these consequences will occur? Could you be underestimating your or others' ability to cope with them? Would you take more responsibility for them than you need to? Would you be unfairly hard on yourself in terms of what it would mean about you as a person if the worst happened? Re-rate your level of fear about the consequences on a 0–100% scale.

Feared consequences worksheet

Date: _____

Obsessional doubt:

_____

Current view	Realistic view

Appendix 4

Behavioural track worksheets*

* Please refer to Chapter 8

ERP – Obsessions and rituals assessment worksheet

Time	Situation (in which you experience the urge to ritualize)	Discomfort in situation (0–100%)	Describe the ritual	Duration (minutes or number of rituals)

ERP – Hierarchy of situations worksheet

Theme category:

Situation (describe the main situations/thoughts/objects or images that provoke your obsessional fears; rank the situations from easier to more difficult)	Baseline discomfort (0–100%)	Tick when discomfort below 20% *

* Use this column for tracking your progress with ERP

ERP – Exposure plan for one situation

Situation:

Hierarchy of steps for reducing ritualizing (rank the steps from easier to more difficult)	Tick when discomfort below 20%*

* Use this column for tracking your progress with your exposure plan.

Working on my negative thinking about exposure

(Complete the first two columns *before* the exposure session and the third column *after*.)

Situation:

What I fear may happen during and following exposure (write down your 'hot thoughts')	*The realistic alternative view (write down the 'cool', realistic answers to your hot thoughts)*	*What actually happened and what I've learned from the experience*

Tracking my discomfort during exposure

Situation:

Date:

Time interval (minutes)	Discomfort (0–100%)
Start	
15 min.	
30 min.	
45min.	
60 min.	
75 min.	
90 min.	

Appendix 5

Relaxation methods

Progressive relaxation therapy (PR)*

Doing progressive relaxation therapy (PR) requires the use of a comfortable chair in a tranquil setting. It would be a good idea for you to record the steps described below on an audio tape or a digital recorder or ask a friend with a comforting voice to record it for you. The person recording should speak in a calm and measured tone, and any of the steps can be repeated if you feel that this is a particular problem area for you.

Remember that relaxation is a skill, so don't be surprised if the steps outlined below aren't helpful the first time. With repeated practice, you'll find that you achieve better results. The challenge is to develop an intimate knowledge of what the sensations of tension in your muscles feel like, and then to learn how to release the tension and relax the muscles.

---

* Adapted from the procedure described in Jones and Hayward (2004)

Try following the steps below.

I'd like you to close your eyes, sit comfortably and try to relax. Scan your body for signs of tension. Now let the tension dissolve and allow your body to sink down into the chair, loose and limp, very loose and limp, and relaxed. Just let your body relax, slowly. Good.

Now, tense your right hand. Make a fist with your right hand. Clench the fist. Feel the tension in your right hand. Feel what it feels like. Good. Now relax your right hand completely. Let it flop down. Feel the relaxation flowing into your right hand. See how different it is to the tension. Your right hand is loose and limp, feeling very relaxed. [Brief pause] Good.

Now, tense your left hand. Make a fist with your left hand. Clench the first. Feel all the tension in your left hand. Good. Now relax your left hand completely. Let it flop down. Feel the relaxation flowing into your left hand. See how different it is to the tension. Your left hand is loose and limp, feeling very relaxed. [Brief pause] Good.

Now, tense your right upper arm. You can do this by touching your right shoulder with your right hand and making your arm very tense. Feel the tension. Good. Now, relax, relax. Just let your right arm relax completely. Experience the feelings of relaxation in your right arm. Your right arm and right hand are very loose, limp and relaxed. [Brief pause] Good.

Now, tense your left upper arm. You can do this by touching your left shoulder with your left hand and making your arm very tense. Feel the tension. Good. Now relax, relax. Just let your left arm relax completely. Experience the feelings of relaxation in your left arm. Your left arm and left hand are very loose, limp and relaxed. [Brief pause] Good.

Now, tense your shoulders. Shrug your shoulders up towards your ears. Your shoulders are very tense. Feel all the tension in your shoulders. [Brief pause] Good. Now relax, relax. Just let your shoulders relax. Your shoulders should be very loose, limp and relaxed, very loose, limp and relaxed. [Brief pause] Good.

Now, I'd like you to relax your neck. Just very gently let your head roll from side to side. Don't do this too vigorously, but just gently roll your neck back and forth and let all those muscles relax. Just let your whole upper body relax. You should feel very loose and limp and relaxed, very loose and limp and relaxed. [Brief pause] Good.

Now, slowly take a deep breath. Hold it (pause about one second) and now let it out. And as the air flows out of your lungs, feel all the tension leaving your body. You feel very loose and limp and relaxed, very loose and limp and relaxed. [Brief pause] Good.

Now, tense up your right foot by curling up your toes. Just feel the tension in your right foot. Experience how that feels. And now relax, relax. Just let your right foot relax. Your right foot should be very loose and limp and relaxed, very loose and limp and relaxed. Feel the relaxation. [Brief pause] Good.

Now, tense up your left foot by curling up your toes. Just feel the tension in your left foot. Experience how that feels. And now relax, relax. Just let your left foot relax. Your left foot should be very loose and limp and relaxed, very loose and limp and relaxed. Feel the relaxation. [Brief pause] Good.

Now, tense up your right leg. Just press down hard with your right heel and tense up your right leg. Feel the tension in your right leg. And now relax, relax. Just let your right leg relax. Your right leg and your right foot should be very loose and limp and relaxed, very loose and limp and relaxed. Experience how that feels. [Brief pause] Good.

Now, tense up your left leg. Just press down hard with your left heel and tense up your left leg. Feel the tension in your left leg. And now relax, relax. Just let your left leg relax. Your left leg and your left foot should be very loose and limp and relaxed, very loose and limp and relaxed. Experience how that feels. [Brief pause] Good.

Now, tense up your stomach. Tighten up all the muscles in your stomach. Feel the tension in your stomach. Now relax, relax. Just let your stomach relax. Your stomach should be very loose and limp and relaxed, very loose and limp and relaxed. Your whole lower body should be loose and limp and relaxed. Feel the relaxation in your lower body. Feel how it spreads through your lower body. [Brief pause] Good.

Now, slowly take a deep breath. Hold it (pause about one second) and now let it out. And as the air flows out of your lungs, feel all the tension leaving your body. You feel very loose and limp and relaxed, very loose and limp and relaxed. [Brief pause] Good.

Now, tense up all the muscles in your forehead. Just wrinkle up your forehead. Feel the tension in your forehead. Now relax, relax. Just let your forehead relax. Your forehead should be very loose and limp and relaxed, very loose and limp and relaxed. [Brief pause] Good.

Now, tense up your eyes. Squeeze your eyes shut tight. Feel the tension in your eyes and in your eyelids. And now relax, relax. Just let your eyes relax. Your eyes should feel very loose and limp and relaxed. Feel the relaxation in your eyes. [Brief pause] Good.

Now, tense up your nose. Wrinkle up your nose. Feel the tension in your nose. And now relax, relax. Just let your nose relax. Your nose should feel very loose and limp and relaxed, very loose and limp and relaxed. Feel that relaxing feeling in your nose. [Brief pause] Good.

Now, tense up your cheeks. Pull back your cheeks in a wide grin. Feel the tension in your cheeks. And now, relax, relax. Just let your cheeks relax. Your cheeks should feel very loose and limp and relaxed, very loose and limp and relaxed. Feel that relaxing feeling in your cheeks. [Brief pause] Good.

Now, finally, tense up your jaw. Clench your teeth and feel the tension in your jaw. And now, relax, relax. Just let your jaw relax. Your jaw should feel very loose and limp and relaxed, very loose and limp and relaxed. Feel that relaxing feeling in your jaw. [Brief pause] Good.

Now, take a deep breath. Hold it (pause for one second), and now let it out. And as the breath leaves your body, feel the tension leaving your body. You feel very loose and limp and relaxed, very loose and limp and relaxed. [Brief pause] Good.

Now, I'm going to count from one to five, and as I count you are going to feel more and more relaxed. If there's any tension anywhere in your body, just let it dissolve away. One. Relax. Two. You feel loose and limp and relaxed all over. Three. Just let the tension leave your body. Your body feels limp and floppy, as if you have no bones at all. Four. Relax. You feel loose and limp and relaxed, very loose and limp and relaxed. Five.

Now you feel relaxed and very comfortable. If there's any remaining tension in your body, just let it slowly dissolve away.

Now, imagine yourself being in the following situation. You're sitting on a deckchair in a big garden on a balmy summer evening. You're all alone; it's very quiet and peaceful. It's so late at night that there are no cars and no people. There's a cool, pleasant breeze and you can hear the sound of leaves gently rustling. There's a scent of summer flowers in the air. You can see a faint glimmer of streetlights through the leaves, but otherwise the garden is dark and silent, there's nobody there. You feel pleasantly tired, just relaxed with nothing to do. You're sitting quietly and peacefully in the chair, enjoying the silence. You look up and see the moon, high up in the sky, lighting up the clouds, and you see a few stars twinkling. It's very peaceful and you feel very relaxed and comfortable. You have nowhere to go, nothing to do, you can just sit there and look up at the moon and the clouds slowly drifting by with the leaves gently rustling in the summer breeze. You feel very comfortable and loose and limp and relaxed. Now you can just sit here and enjoy the beautiful evening, comfortable and at peace.

Abdominal breathing exercise*

This is a shorter relaxation exercise than progressive relaxation, and can therefore be used more flexibly in hectic life situations when and where you need it. Follow the steps below.

Place your hand on your abdomen right beneath your ribcage. Now, inhale slowly and deeply through your nose into the 'bottom' of your lungs. Send the air down as far 'below' as is possible. If you are breathing from your abdomen, your hand placed on your stomach should rise and your chest should move only slightly. This happens because the diaphragm, which is the muscle separating the lung cavity from the abdominal cavity, moves downward. By moving downward, it causes the muscles surrounding the abdominal cavity to push outwards.

After taking a deep breath, pause for a moment and then exhale slowly through your nose or your mouth, whatever you prefer. Make sure that you exhale fully. As you exhale, allow your body to release your tension and just flop down and go limp. It may be helpful to visualize the tension as a dark mist gently being released from your lungs as you breathe out. Try to keep your thoughts focused on your breathing and if you find that your mind wanders, just gently bring your focus back to your breathing in the present.

Now do ten deep abdominal breaths. Try to keep your breathing smooth and regular without gulping in air or exhaling all at once. Pause briefly at the end of each exhalation. The process should go like this: Slow inhale ... pause ... Slow exhale ('one'); Slow inhale ... pause ... Slow exhale ('two').

* Adapted from the procedure described in Bourne (1990)

And so on, up until 'ten' (or you may count backwards from ten). You may also prefer not to count and simply continue the exercise until you feel sufficiently relaxed. If you feel dizzy at any point, stop for 30 seconds and then start again.

You may choose to extend the exercise by doing two or three sets of abdominal breaths. Five full minutes of abdominal breathing will have a pronounced effect on anxiety reduction.

References

Aardema, F. and O'Connor, K. (2007). The menace within: obsessions and the self. *Journal of Cognitive Psychotherapy*, 32: 182–97.

Baer, L. (2000). *Getting Control: Overcoming Your Obsessions and Compulsions*. New York, Plume.

Beck, A.T. (1998). *Love Is Never Enough*. New York, Harper & Row.

Beck, J.S. (1996). *Cognitive Therapy Worksheet Packet*. Bala Cynwyd, PA, Beck Institute for Cognitive Therapy and Research.

Bourne, E.J. (1990). *The Anxiety & Phobia Workbook*. New Harbinger, Oakland.

Brown, R.A., Abrantes, A.M., Strong, D.R., Mancebo, M.C., Menard, J., Rasmussen, S.A. and Greenberg, B.D. (2007). A pilot study of moderate-intensity aerobic exercise for obsessive-compulsive disorder. *Journal of Nervous and Mental Disease*, 195: 514–20.

Foa, E.B. and Wilson, R. (2001). *Stop Obsessing! How to Overcome Your Obsessions and Compulsions*. New York, Bantam Books.

Gómez-Pinilla, F. (2008). Brain foods: the effects of nutrients on brain function. *Nature Reviews Neuroscience*, 9: 568–78.

Greenberger, D. and Padesky, C.A. (1995). *Mind over Mood: Change How You Feel by Changing the Way You Think*. New York, Guilford Press.

Jones, S. and Hayward, P. (2004). *Coping with Schizophrenia.* Oxford, Oneworld.

Muris, P., Merckelbach, H. and Clavan, M. (1997). Abnormal and normal compulsions. *Behaviour Research and Therapy,* 35: 249–52.

O'Connor, K., Aardema, F. and Pélissier, M. (2005). *Beyond Reasonable Doubt – Reasoning Processes in Obsessive-Compulsive Disorder and Related Disorders.* Chichester, Wiley.

Pirie, M. (2006). *How to Win Every Argument: the Use and Abuse of Logic.* London, Continuum.

Rachman, S. and De Silva, P. (1978). Abnormal and normal obsessions. *Behaviour Research and Therapy,* 16: 233–48.

Schwartz, J.M. (1998). Neuroanatomical aspects of cognitive-behavioural therapy response in obsessive-compulsive disorder: an evolving perspective on brain and behaviour. *British Journal of Psychiatry,* 173 (35S): 38–44.

Schwartz, J.M., Stoessel, P.W., Baxter, L.R., Martin, K.M. and Phelps, M.E. (1996). Systematic change in cerebral glucose metabolic rate after successful behaviour modification treatment of obsessive compulsive disorder. *Archives of General Psychiatry,* 53: 109–13.

Van Oppen, P. and Arntz, A. (1994). Cognitive therapy for obsessive-compulsive disorder. *Behaviour Research and Therapy,* 32: 79–87.

Williams, J.M.G., Teasdale, J.D., Segal Z.V. and Kabar-Zinn, J. (2004). *The Mindful Way through Depression: Freeing Yourself from Chronic Unhappiness.* New York, Guilford Press.

Wu, K.D., Clark, L.A. and Watson, D. (2006). Relations between obsessive-compulsive disorder and personality: beyond Axis I–Axis II comorbidity. *Anxiety Disorders,* 20: 695–717.

Young, J.E. and Klosko, J. (1998). *Reinventing Your Life: How to Break Free from Negative Life Patterns.* USA, Penguin Putnam, Inc.

Index